Kundalini Awakening

Generate Power Through Chakra Meditation, and Healing Your Body

(Practical Techniques and Exercises to Develop Awareness and Spiritual Power)

Raynes Woods

Published By **Oliver Leish**

Raynes Woods

Kundalini Awakening: Generate Power Through Chakra Meditation, and Healing Your Body (Practical Techniques and Exercises to Develop Awareness and Spiritual Power)

ISBN   978-1-998769-51-3

No part of this guidebook shall be reproduced in any form without permission in writing from the publisher except in the case of brief quotations embodied in critical articles or reviews.

Legal & Disclaimer

The information contained in this ebook is not designed to replace or take the place of any form of medicine or professional medical advice. The information in this ebook has been provided for educational & entertainment purposes only.

The information contained in this book has been compiled from sources deemed reliable, and it is accurate to the best of the Author's knowledge; however, the Author cannot guarantee its accuracy and validity and cannot be held liable for any errors or omissions. Changes are periodically made to this book. You must consult your doctor or get professional medical advice before using any of the suggested remedies, techniques, or information in this book.

Table Of Contents

Introduction

All people have Kundalini. The people who have this knowledge are able to use more of their inherent potential and transform others and the world. It is because this energy, which is nothing but the force of evolution, has been placed on the base of each of our spines.

Kundalini is a power that has been well known by ancient people. Over thousands of years, the knowledge of how to activate this energy has only been available to a select few and never to others. Recently, Kundalini masters began to share the information with "outsiders".

Kundalini knowledge has been poured out in response to modern needs. Science and technology advanced, and materialism became more powerful. Spirituality was considered a relic from the "ignorant", past. People became distracted from their inventions and began to separate themselves from nature, their souls.

The Spirit may be what entices people to the spiritual, which is something many old religions attempted but didn't achieve. Kundalini awakening may be one of many ways to get back to the divine. It brings joy as well as a greater ability to access the energy flowing throughout creation. This allows you to see everything in its true context.

This book will provide a simple guide for awakening your Kundalini. You can find a lot of additional information online that will help you understand this energy better. This book could be your Spirit's gift to you. It contains only the essential information you need to awaken and do it immediately.

Chapter 1: What Is Kundalini Exactly?

Kundali can be described as the energy or consciousness of Kundali. This is a spiritual and psycho energy that lives in the resting body. The term literally translates to "annular/circle" and was also used as a name for snakes in 12th century.

Its origins are the yogic belief corporeal energies are real and reside in the body of a person, especially at their base. Kundalini can awaken if one connects to his soul and decides to find the truth within.

The Kundali represents a sleeping snake or a goddess at one's spine, where all power and energy is found. It also represents a libidinal, or instinctive force.

Kundalini became popular in the 1970's. But, research shows that many, including Carl Jung, a well-known Psychologer, knew about Kundalini even before that time. Their knowledge of Sanskrit and Greek teachings helped them to be more aware of the phenomenon. Kundalini, incidentally, has been used in technical terms in most Shakti/Durga writings back to the 11th-century. Yoga Upanishads use it to demonstrate their superior power.

Kundalini can be found in all people. It is present at the base or spine of the body. This energy, also known as the Kundalini or spiritual energy, is more subtle than the physical. No matter what meditation, spiritual or religious tradition, awakening this energy is essential for spiritual advancement, unfoldment and realization.

What does it serve?

You might be wondering why Kundali has to be awakened. Here's what you should know.

Kundalini means to cleanse your mind and body. It is a way to detoxify yourself without the need to make green juices and change your diet. Kundali works in a way that, once awakened by you, it will clean and refresh your body for 24 hours every day, seven days a semaine.

It can also cleanse your chakras. This is the area of your subconscious mind that houses vital energy and your life force. If your Kundalini doesn't get awakened, you will not be able take full advantage of your chakras.

You will be reunited with the Supreme Being by awakening Kundalini. Kundalini can be portrayed as a goddess. Once it awakens, it will move toward your head, where Lord Shiva, or The Supreme Being, resides. It can be said that you now feel connected to the Supreme being because you have discovered a level of divinity not available to most people. Kundalini's awakening will lead to the realization of many important things.

If the Supreme Being calls, you will be returned as a purified, whole person. You also experience a new sense of peace. This will allow for you to live a more satisfying life.

Chapter 2: Chakras

"The Kundalini dwells within the Muladhara (1st chakra). When it is awakened, it travels along the Sushumna nerve and then through the centres Svadhisthana, Manipura (second/third Chakras), and finally reaches the head." Sri Ramakrishna (Annac 2019, 2019)

Different areas of the body are known as Chakras. They are where energy is concentrated, collected and used. These areas of concentrated energies can be beneficial for the individual's spiritual, mental, and physical well-being (Siddhayatan). The chakras function correctly when people are in balance with themselves and others. Kundalini yoga and meditation are two examples of Kundalini yoga. These are the energy centres that are either negatively affected by the kinked snake or stretched out within the spine. Once the snake is stretched all the way from the base down to the crown, the chakras should be functioning properly.

The individual might experience mental or physical distresses if they are out of balance, misused incorrectly, or not using the chakras correctly. To put it another way, if the serpent is coiled or kinked at different places, it could indicate that the chakras have not been balanced and can reflect on the individual's negative and difficult emotions. It could indicate that your chakras have not been functioning properly or are out of balance.

There are seven types of chakras in an individual. These are energy areas that aid the individual in their daily lives. Each of seven chakras can represent a different level in consciousness, awareness, mindfulness, or awareness. They also represent a different type of energy within the individual (Hridaya. n.d). Each chakra corresponds to a specific part or element of the body.

It is recommended to imagine yourself as a person lying cross-legged, on the ground, with the chakras in place. This pose will help you understand how meditation works.

Muladhara Chakra

The first chakra represents the foundation. The root chakra, also known as the muladhara, can be found in the sitting bone or anal area. This chakra symbolizes foundation. It is the part of an individual that touches the ground. The chakra that is open means the individual feels calm and confident when it is being utilized effectively. The chakra that isn't working properly or closed can cause an individual to feel weak and incompetent. They might also feel scared or threatened by the world around them as they lack the strength to take on the challenges ahead.

The element of ground and the colour red are some symbols that are associated to the root chakra. These symbols are chosen since they usually signify power, and the earth element is the ground. The root chakra is what connects us to the earth and gives us physical power.

This chakra can be developed when an individual is aged between one and seven. Because between these years, the individual is primarily developing their connection to the physical world and themselves, it is believed that this is the best time to build this chakra.

The root chakra is associated with a mantra. Although there are many variations and versions of this mantra, it can be summarized as: "I cannot develop or grow from an unsteady foundational basis" (Cameron. 2020).

Understanding the seven chakras begins with understanding the root chakra. As it is, and as was just mentioned, the foundation upon the building of one's energy.

Svadhisthanachakra

The sacral chakra, also known as Svadhisthana is the second chakra. As the root chakra is located in the pelvis, genital or genital area of a seated individual, it can be seen just above it. This chakra allows us empathy with others and to name and identify our emotions. This chakra governs sexual energies. When this chakra has been used correctly, it is able to bring balance to the emotions. The individual does not feel overwhelmed or lacking in emotion. They will also enjoy a satisfying sexual life. It does not necessarily mean the person is participating in sexual activities regularly and continuously. However, it does mean that their sexual needs have been met (Cameron and 2020).

This chakra can also be a source of extreme mood swings and depression. The individual might also feel sexually frustrated.

This chakra is most commonly developed between the ages 14 and eight years. This is because the individual's sexual and emotional development takes place during those years. This is when an individual's emotional consciousness develops and can recognize that others can influence their emotions.

This chakra is a complex one with its own symbols and mantras. For example, this chakra is colored orange while the element is water. The mantra for chakra oh is "I always respect others but never before myself" (Cameron - 2020).

Manipura Chakra

The third chakra is located in the solar plexus (or the stomach of the seated individual). It is often called the Manipura and the navel chakra. The chakra in this area functions much like the core abdominal muscle muscles. The solar chakra is responsible for self-esteem development and self-worth. The individual might feel overwhelmed by self-doubt or low self-esteem if they are not using their solar chakra properly. The chakra that is working well will make the person feel more confident and free in every situation.

The color yellow and the element fire are usually used as symbols for the solarplexus chakra. Additionally, the solar plexus chakra is typically developed between 15-

21 years of age. These are the years when individuals form their identity, self-esteem, and personal character.

The mantra to their solar plexus is "self-love comes when I accept all aspects of myself". (Cameron, 2020). This mantra is intended to encourage individuals not to place their needs before their own. This is not meant as a way to encourage selfishness. It's meant to be focused on the person first, so self-love and compassion can result in productivity and compassion for others.

Anahata Chakra

The Anahta chakra, also known as the heart chakra, is the next chakra. This chakra can be found just above the solar center and the heart. Although it might seem obvious that this chakra influences how we love and are open to receiving love, this does not mean intimate or romantic relationships. This chakra refers to all forms of love. This chakra should be used correctly to allow the individual to freely share their love with others, and also to accept love. If the heart chakra does not function properly, an individual may feel unworthy and not worthy of love. They may also not be showing their love to others. This chakra also regulates our ability and willingness to love others. This means that our ability to love ourselves can be affected if it isn't fully awake.

The mantra for this chakra is "When I love me, loving other people comes easily" (Cameron. 2020). This mantra addresses both the issue and the importance of loving others. It is also a focus on the heart chakra. For this chakra's symbols, the element is air and the colour is green.

The most common time this chakra develops is between the ages 22 and 28. This is due to the fact that this is when an individual discovers different types of love. At this age, they are more confident about themselves and have their own ways of loving themselves. They are likely to have a certain type of love and support for their family and friends.

Vishuddha Chakra

The fifth chakra, which is located in the throat of an individual, is called Vishuddha. This chakra, named Vishuddha, is responsible for our communication skills. A person should be able to communicate their feelings, ideas and creativity to others when the chakra has been properly opened. They can also speak up and share their truth with those around. The chakra may become blocked if the individual has difficulty speaking up about what is happening in their heart and mind. The chakra may also be affected if an individual opens their chakra too often. This can cause communication problems, such as communication that doesn't have a filter or is free from communication. Therefore, the mantra for the chakra's is "I speak the truth." I speak the truth. (Cameron - 2020).

This chakra is typically developed between the ages of 29 and 35. Again, this is due to the fact that these years are when an individual is able to establish a steady job and build relationships with other people that require clear communication. The symbols of the chakra are usually made from light blue. The element, sound and music, is the colour. This element may not be obvious given that the chakra deals with auditory and vocal communication.

Ajna Chkra

The Ajna (third eye chakra) is the sixth chakra. This chakra is found in the middle of the forehead near the eyes. This chakra focuses on visualization. This chakra is not just focused on visualization of the here and now, but also visualizations for what's next or what's ahead. Person who uses their third eye chakra can keep their future predictions in check. They can see the future, anticipate what is going to happen, and are flexible enough to accept any changes. The person with their third eye closed may worry about the future, and be out of touch with the world. This chakra, which is the oldest of the first six chakras, develops most rapidly when an individual is 36 to 42 years old. This is because they have gained wisdom from their experiences and years. They no longer live life through their senses. Instead, they experience it through their experiences. Wisdom is generally associated with a female or royal gender. Therefore, the symbolic color associated to this chakra can be either a deep blue or a purple. The symbol for the chakra's symbolic element is light. It is light that illuminates and illuminates the reality.

Finally, this definition allows us to create the mantra for the Chakra: "I am open-minded to exploring what cannot been seen." (Cameron. 2020).

Sahasrara Chakra

The crown chakra or Sahasrara is the last chakra. The chakra is located at the crown, which is the highest point of an individual's head, as the name suggests. If this chakra is properly opened, it is possible to access a higher and more peaceful state of consciousness and mindfulness. It is rare that anyone can open this chakra completely and correctly. This chakra's mantra reads, "I am the center for love & light." (Cameron - 2020). The element is divine consciousness. The symbolic colour is blue. However, this chakra represents inner peace and perfection. If an individual is in this state, all of their possibilities are possible.

Although it is rare for people to reach this level, this chakra is usually not developed until one is in their late 40's. Kundalini yoga practice has made it possible for individuals to reach this level. Many yogis consider the crown chakra not to be a true Chakra. This is because it is more of a state than a point of energy.

* * *

As I mentioned, someone can feel blocked if one or several chakras are out-of-balance. These exercises can help you open your chakras and teach you how to use them. Refer to Chapter 10 for the different exercises.

Chapter 3: The Principles Of Kundalini Yoga

These principles were based on an ancient system, yet they still have relevance to our modern lives. This spiritual energy begins at your spine and is called the "process of awakening". It refers to how the energy spreads from your spine to your head through time and practice.

Kundalini is described by the metaphysical side of the practices as an awakening snake. It emits an energy, called chakra, which takes refuge at 7 points in your body during growth. According to the methodology, the chakra energy rises through the body the same way air fills the lungs. Then oxygenated bloods are dispersed throughout the vital organs of the body when you exhale.

It is possible to go beyond the first 6 chakras, and reach the 7th through the "golden cable". Legend says that the cord connects pituitary, pineal, and other glands. This is significant as these glands are said to have been responsible in part for awakening the conscious brain of an individual. These glands are involved in Kundalini Yoga as well as many other ancient and contemporary teachings. You can access them by seeing the world as it really is instead of what you hope or imagine it to be. This practice is known as the golden chord, and it is the key for your awakening.

Kundalini Yoga blends three different, more specific yoga-related spiritual practices. Each yoga focuses upon a particular aspect of the human experience. This includes devotion (Bhakti), power and mental fortitude combined with control (Raja). Each offers an avenue to attain a higher consciousness as well as a way to unleash your creative potential. These practices are a practical technology to the conscious mind.

Kundalini Yoga allows you to harness your inner power and release the debts of karma. To put it in western terms, being freed of one's karmic obligations is basically the same as being forgiven and released from all the mistakes you have made. It will ensure that your soul feels peaceful and that your soul will remain content long after you pass away. It is an intriguing concept that adds another spiritual benefit to Kundalini Yoga.

Chapter 4: Benefits From Kundalini Awakening

It is now time to understand why it is important to use your chakras. There are many decisions that you have to make in your life. The most important thing you can do is assess how important you place your well-being. Kundalini is a tool that can help you spiritually heal and grow.

Kundalini is a practice that can bring you beyond the limits of time and space. By doing this, you can experience your true self and soul at a whole different level. This can help you to increase your security as well as strength. Kundalini-Awakening can bring about other benefits.

1. Sacred Chant. Many chakras can heal themselves using sacred chants. A mantra, rhythm, or breath can have positive effects on your health and well-being. It

can also bring joy and peace to the soul. Naad Yoga is the sacred sound. The vibrations of the voice can have a positive influence on the body, the mind and the spirit. You can even alter the chemicals in the brain by making a sound.

2. Kundalini Yoga & Kundalini Yoga: Inner Soul Guidance You must learn how to hear your intuition. Every person has a voice. It is up to each individual to choose to hear it. By clearing your mind, and especially your subconscious mind you can learn to listen to what you think without having to rely on others. In this way, you can be present and hear your intuition. Practice makes you more able to make decisions and face them.

3. Karma

Kundalini is believed by many to take you out of the cycle and bring you back into your true self. Kundalini Kriyas can be accessed by practicing Kundalini. Your positive intention will grow as you practice. These are exercises to help you eliminate karma. You will find yourself more in touch with your subconscious and more intuitive when you practice. When you do this you will be able to walk the path of Dharma and not live in accordance with karma.

4. Spiritual Chain

Kundalini has a long history of being taught. It was first taught by a master to the student. Kundalini Yoga classes include the chanting of "Ong Namoguru Dev Namo." It will allow you to connect with spiritual masters in times past. The Golden Chain is the name given to this lineage. It will give you spiritual awareness and guarantee that the Kundalini teachings will be unadulterated.

5. Emotional Balance

The truth is, balancing Kundalini also means that you are balancing your hormones, your nervous system, your glands, your blood and your subconscious. When you awaken your Kundalini you will find the power to choose how you react to your thoughts and feelings, instead of reacting. You will have greater awareness throughout your day. As you practice, you'll also be able to let your emotions go. It is no longer enough to react emotionally. If you can develop a positive mindset, you might find it easier to live a happier and more fulfilling life. Acting instead of reacting is the key.

6. No More Negativity

When you practice awakening your Kundalini, your aura will grow. This is the energy that surrounds you. Its primary function is to detect any positive or harmful emotions. Your aura may be weak at this point. It is easy to allow negative influences into your life if your aura weakens. By strengthening your aura, you can keep yourself centered and discover your true identity.

7. New Lifestyle

Life is full of excuses that make us miserable. Kundalini Yoga can be adapted to busy lifestyles. It is quick and easy to do, yet still be effective. It's a yoga that fits into many lifestyles. There are many benefits to attending weekly or biweekly. There are yoga teachings that can help you change your life. You can do yoga to improve your communication, hygiene, or child-rearing skills.

8. Relax

Kundalini yoga can help to strengthen your nervous and immune system, as mentioned previously. You may be more vulnerable to stress if your nervous systems is weak. Yoga can teach you to relax in a way you have never experienced before. You might find yoga helps you reach a state of relaxation that allows you to feel completely relaxed. Regular practice of yoga can improve your stress resilience and increase your stamina.

9. Community

This is not a solo journey. Yoga is a great way to bring people together who share similar beliefs. This can be a powerful tool for you as you journey along your consciousness path. Kundalini Yoga studios and centers are available to welcome you into their community. When you meditate and chant with others, you'll create a community. It's also beneficial to have other people who will help you make positive life changes.

10. Befriending your Soul

Kundalini can help you get in touch with your inner self as you practice it. As you practice Kundalini, you will gradually discover more about the depths of your soul. You can then connect with the universe and your soul. More practice will help you to become one with the Infinite. This experience can help to forget your own insecurity about being who you are. This will help you let go the past and allow you to manifest your dreams in a healthy way.

Chapter 5: Dangers Associated With Awakening Kundalini

Finally, let's talk about some possible dangers when you try to awaken Kundalini. These aren't intended to scare you.

After you've walked all the ways toward Kundalini-Awakening, your final destination will be bliss, awareness and infinite love.

Here are some instances to keep an eye on:

Overeating or loss of appetite

People may experience difficulty adjusting to Kundalini exercises.

Because yoga is a 2 to 3 hour practice, a person shouldn't eat heavy before it. Some people become so busy that they want to eat as soon as they can, but then they find themselves with a problem of appetite due to the position they have taken.

Disrupted sleeping patterns

In order to awake Kundalini, you put your body through a series of experiences. Your body may experience a lot of different sensations, which can cause you to have difficulty sleeping or to oversleep.

Altered States of Consciousness

It is common for people to feel like they are in a state of trance.

It's possible to feel as though you're in some kind of trance, but this is what you'd do.

Remember that you are creating your own reality so you should feel this distortion.

Sensitivity of Touch, Light and Sounds

Another thing that you might notice is a rise in your awareness to all things around you. This is due to tapping into your subconscious. It's the reason you start to see things as more than they are.

Pains in the neck/back

Kundalini is at the base your spine. Therefore, if you are able to engage in yoga and other yogic activities that stimulate it, you'd feel tension in your muscles. Also, you would feel pain in your neck and back areas which connect to the spine.

Resting a bit is key. You can visit a doctor if the pain does not go away.

Mood Swings

There may be occasions when your mood swings are unpredictable, like if medication has been taken. You might find yourself easily annoyed or crying at the smallest provocation.

This is because your subconscious mind opens up, and you are able to feel more. This is how you feel conflicted and may even feel like you aren't yourself anymore.

People can experience an emotional numbness in some cases. It is as if they feel nothing for whatever's going on. This is because their subconscious mind has enabled them to separate from their mind and from their hearts.

Sometimes, an individual may be more antisocial than others while awakening Kundalini.

Paranoia can also occur when you see or hear things that aren't there. These are symptoms of tapping on various chakras.

An irregular heartbeat/increased blood pressure

Sometimes, you may feel your heartbeat irregularly or your heart rate is palpitating. This can happen when you're praying a lot and doing exercises that place a lot on the blood.

Also, you may experience headaches, migraines or pressure on the skull. Sometimes intense heat or cold can be experienced along with some tingling sensations.

Just a reminder...

Keep in mind, unless you feel very uncomfortable or are certain that something is wrong, these are all experiences that Kundalini will allow you to experience true bliss.

However, if you don't feel like doing the exercises anymore, you may stop.

Chapter 6: Meditation For Kundalini Energy

Kundalini Meditation

This meditation will awaken your Kundalini energy, and allow you to feel balanced.

How to Use This Meditation

The awakening meditation should be practiced at least once daily. You can awaken your Kundalini Energy for the day by using it early in the morning. It helps you to balance your energies so you can continue living a peaceful and intentional life.

The meditation requires a specific breathing pattern. This will be described in the script below. When you combine this breathing with the reflection, you'll likely notice that your natural breathing rhythm will be influenced by the meditation.

When this happens, Kundalini energy will infuse your everyday life. The energy will work naturally to infuse the renewed breathing pattern.

As previously stated, the meditation should take around 15 minutes. It is easy and simple to incorporate into your day. It will help to de-stress, awaken and empower you to approach your day.

Kundalini awakening as well as meditation are journeys. This means that you must make a commitment to these practices every single day. However, you shouldn't feel guilty or ashamed if you don't use them every day. But you should try your best to not miss any days. Kundalini energy is the best way to keep your practice going strong. It will also help you continue to awaken your Kundalini energies. You'll gain more power from this practice the more you commit.

Meditation

Start by finding your centre. Begin by bringing awareness to the tip end of your nose. Next, drop it down into your center where your solar chakra is. After you have done this, use your breath as your focus. Your mind should be able to focus on rhythmic breathing and not the chatter. It is a good moment to relax, inhale deeply, and then fill up your lungs. Inhale and empty your throat. Next, fill your lungs with air. Keep going without stopping. Simply breathe. Even though you can't get your heart beat to stop at a different speed, steady rhythmic breathing can calm your heart and restore harmony.

Keep breathing and you will find a comfortable rhythm. One, two. three. and four. Continue to let this rhythm flow gently through your lungs and keep your focus on your center.

You might begin to notice movements in your lower belly while you breathe. This indicates that your energy is ready to be awakened. You might feel this movement as a sensation, or a fluttering feeling of energy. You can feel it and be aware of your inner world.

After that, you can continue to count four. Let the energy flow up your spine, allowing it to begin to rise. This energy rises from the sacral chakra. It flows up your spine purifying it with your life force energy. It is better to simply observe the process unfolding than visualize it. You can focus on the energy rising. Set the intention to draw that energy up to your spine. Continue to let it rise up until it reaches the crown.

Breathe in for a few minutes. In, two, three, four... out, two, three, four.

Once the process is completed, take a moment to relax into the sensations. After the process is complete, you can draw your attention back into the room and become more aware of the surroundings. Allow yourself to feel how this sensation remains within you despite the fact you are being awakened into the energy in the room. Keep this energy with your throughout the day. It can inspire you, guide your steps, and keep you awake as you go about your daily activities.

Tantra Meditation

Tantra can also be used to awaken Kundalini-energy. If tantra is something you haven't heard of, or used it before, you will be intrigued to find out more. Tantra is based largely on sexual life-giving energy as well as its ability to infuse the bodies with awakened Energies. We will go deeper into tantra in order to fully understand its magic and help you achieve your Kundalini awakening. In case you are not familiar with tantra, or don't understand what it does, let us start by looking at tantra. Tantra is an ancient, secretive, and powerful spiritual technique that originated in India. Tantra was derived from the Indian language "Sanskrit", and consists of two root word: Tan, which is about body, and Tra, that's about a process to expand.

Tantra is a spiritual practice that uses the body to achieve spiritual enlightenment. Contrary to other spiritual methods which consider the body dirty, tantra sees the body a divine temple. Tantra employs sex as an instrument to improve awareness and consciousness. Tantra is a combination of yoga and sex. It reaches a new dimension. This new dimension can be more profound and subtle than a human mind can ever imagine. In tantra, the practitioner conducts many experiments inside the human body. This is how experience, observations and the outcome of these systematic experiments reveal all that is true about existence. This truth can lead to liberation if it is understood by the ignorant mind. Tanta is the ability to merge mind, body, and energy to achieve a higher consciousness level. Tantra includes the use of sex. This instrument can be used to awaken when it is done with total awareness. Tantra is a powerful meditation that dissolves the physical and mental boundaries. It can remove all your inner blockages. It can relax the body, open the heart, and bring the mind into focus. Tantra isn't just a simple technique you can use to fulfill your bodily needs. Tantra is spiritual practice that awakens your core and combines your whole self in it. Tantra can be described as a journey of energy that takes you from the ground to the infinite.

About Tantra

Tantra is a ritualistic, spiritual practice that is rooted both in Hinduisms and Buddhism. This mystical text is as old as the 6th-13th centuries. Many people believe tantra refers to sex when they hear it. Although it does involve sexual energies, the practice is performed in a very ritualistic and intentional way to offer a particular set of benefits. Tantra was sexualized in Western culture, however, since its introduction at the turn of the 19th century.

Tantra includes sexual energy. However, it uses the body for spiritual awakenings. This can be achieved by a series of rituals and chanting that leads to transcending.

How Tantra Impacts Kundalini

While Kundalini can be considered harmless, Western society views it as sexual energy. Some people believe it is rooted sexually and it could be considered taboo. This is however a cultural bias, which North Americans allowed to exist because they approached the subject from a non-liberal standpoint of sexual pleasure.

Kundalini is considered a tantric discipline. It awakens Kundalini Energy by using specific sacred words, hand gestures, and ingenious yoga poses.

Kundalini also incorporates tantra, which is a way to use the body to attain liberation. Kundalini energy is often restricted when our bodies are not awakened. When we awaken, however, our bodies are released and we feel a greater sense relaxation, pure energy flow, peace, and calm.

The Practice of Tantra in Kundalini Awakening

Tantra in Kundalini awakened should only be performed with an extremely powerful teacher who has also mastered their inner state. These tantric teachers will share their yoga techniques with you. The sequences require two people to perform the pose. This is crucial for the awakening of Kundalini Energies.

Tantric Kundalini yoga practices are similar to traditional Kundalini yoga. Their primary difference is the incorporation of another being. The process is extremely powerful, as both the beings are energetically charged and awakened. This practice is best done between a male and female. This allowed for a balanced integration of masculine as well as feminine energies that ultimately leads to the desired outcome.

Tantric Kundalini is not something you can do on your own. You should consult a teacher. Many can suffer from crippling experience due to the intense energy of awakening. Kundalini Energy isn't bad or good, but it does make it more difficult to enjoy the powerful energy.

Pranayama Meditation

The Kundalini rises. Chakras are located along Sushumna Nadi. The Sushumna Nadi (physically located in your spinal cord) is a major prana channel. This allows you to breathe energy through your body. However, there are many other major and minor nadi. Many of these minor nadi come from the Kama, which is very close to the Muldahara, the Kundalini's resting place. If prana flows well and is purposefully combined with this whole system of nadis, the chakras will be awakened.

Prana awareness is primarily in the form and function of breath. Pranayama or disciplined breathing exercises are essential to balance the Nadi and encourage prana to flow through them. This will allow the Kundalini to rise and the chakras to awaken. Pranayama can regulate prana as well as the nadis. It should be done consistently, but not to the point where it becomes exhaustion or uncomfortable. It's usually done in the morning while doing an asana (described here).

Pranayama can be practiced in many ways. A guru is required to help you do it properly and get the best results. You will need to do extensive research before you even attempt to learn. A lot of pranayama activities involve balancing prana throughout the body. This can be done through simple practices like inhaling slowly through one nostril then exhaling out the second. Or more difficult practices such as holding the breath for as long possible and then exhaling into one nostril.

Inner Vision Meditation

Your inner vision will be required for this meditation. Your words are vibratory, so the imagery you use will be vibratory. You can use any image that lifts your energy. To find the images that bring you joy and hope, try out some of them. For help, try picturing warm and golden sunlight. Your inner vision may begin to show you other things than what we'll discuss. This is acceptable as long as it's uplifting.

Find a place you feel comfortable in, where you won't be disturbed for a while. Close your eyes and feel the sensations in your body. Allow yourself to adjust to a supported and comfortable position.

Focus on your breath. Don't try changing it. You might still be able to notice the changes occurring on their own. It could get slower or more deep. It might also become more rapid. It will do what it wants. You can let it be. Just watch your breath and notice how it feels as you inhale and exhale.

If you find your mind drifting during meditation, simply bring it back towards your breath. Be calm and let your mind wander. You will feel great when you return to your breathe. Allow your breathing time to relax.

Once you have relaxed and focusing on your breathing, picture yourself standing underneath the warmth and healing light of a golden sun. This is a state of awareness. This is the essence you and all living beings. It's all encompassing love. It is the purest form love. It shines brighter then any other light you have ever seen. It is brighter than a thousand diamonds.

Allow this light flow into your head, and let it spread throughout your body. Accept the light that it brings to you. It cares about your best interests. The light that spreads through your body fills every tissue and organ of your body. It is absorbed into your memories and thoughts, and it fills them with healing. It will help to take the lessons from your experiences.

This golden light floods your crown chakra. It then spreads to your third eye, opening your heart to the truth.

This warm, healing light falls into your neck and your throat chakra. It balances your energy and unlocks your freedom. It flows from your shoulders to your wrists, fingers, wrists, and hands. It runs through your fingers and returns to the earth.

The fifth chakra is where you feel the light. It reaches your heart and fills your life with love. It pools in the heart and flows outwards. It continues to travel along your chest, back, and front.

The light fills up the solar plexus and your ribs. This area contains your childhood memories, your teen years, and your interactions with your parents. All of these are made fresh and given space, love, softness,, and space. You now realize that you had a Divine companion who accompanied you through everything. This could be a Guardian Angel (or Jesus, Buddha or Love), depending on your choice. This Presence was always there and will be with you in all of your difficulties.

This light continues to fill you with its warmth and light, reaching your sacral chakra. It embraces the child within you. The light tells your inner child that you are proud of him or her. Your inner child is told that there hasn't been any wrong. They only imagined the things they did. Your inner child, your whole self, is beautiful and complete. They are safe and loved.

The golden light continues its journey down to your root chakra. It then spills out in all directions. The light helps you to see the connection between your love for family and other people on Earth. This light is awakening wisdom.

The light heals every thing it touches. All parts of your body are being filled with the light. The light flows down your legs to exit your feet into the Earth.

This pure light flows from the tops of your head down to the tips your toes, filling you with it. All levels are being washed in this golden light. Anything that doesn't serve you will be removed leaving behind a warm feeling of love. Relax and let go.

You can stay here for up to five minutes.

You will experience the light as you are one with it. Your body will dissolve into the light. You will feel the light's freedom. You have unlimited potential and are unbounded. Because you are light, your creativity can be unlimited. You can do all things. You can travel in all directions and you are one of all things.

Asana

Asana, or yoga asana, is what most people think of when they think about it. There are hundreds of different asana. It is also easy to learn the correct way to perform them. While it is unnecessary to detail each asana here, it's important to understand their relation to Kundalini awakening.

Pranayama works best when it is done in the asana position. Asana assists in focusing the mind by controlling your body. It promotes circulation and physical health that are necessary for prana movement to be free and Kundalini's awakening. Kundalini awakening can be made possible by bodily focus. It helps control the physical attachments and discomforts that cause worldly problems. For Kundalini awakening however, some poses are more effective than others. Simple poses like the lotus and similar sitting postures are very beneficial. Also, the topsy turvy and all members poses, which require balance on the shoulders and head, are extremely helpful.

Asana is the best place to start your journey toward Kundalini awakening. They provide the foundation that prepares the mind and body for the journey toward Kundalini awakening. These exercises should be considered more than a routine. It is important to practice regularly and to remain focused on the actions of the body. Not only will you be able to hold these poses for longer periods of time, but your mind will develop the ability to remain still and calm, without any distractions.

Chapter 7: Chakras Healing

Hakras are energy centers within the body that help regulate almost all of the body's processes. They include organ function, immune system, and feelings.

But exactly what is chakra healing?

It can aid in the re-balancing of the flow energy (prana), and improve your general health. This particular therapy works in a similar way to a spring cleaning for your energy system. It unblocks or reactivates and rebalances your chakras, creating a pathway for higher consciousness and greater health.

"Chakra" in Sanskrit means "wheel", and it refers the many power wheels that we have throughout our body. 7 of these are large chakras that align at the backbone with the crown's base. Every person is made up of organs and nerves. They also serve as an important link to the more abstract mental, spiritual and emotionally states.

Our physical, mental, spiritual, and emotional well-being depends on our ability to maintain our chakras open. If we are ill, it is likely that one or more chakras become blocked. This could happen either through physical injury, or by more esoteric issues.

The Chakras

The very first Chakra (Muladhara), represents security and stability.

The next (Svadhisthana), or the sexual chakra of ours is located above our pubic bone. It controls both our creativity and sexual power.

Manipura is the last and most important of all the spiritual beings. It is the source of our personal power.

The Anahata middle and fourth chakras are the heart chakras. This is where you find connection and love.

The 5th (Vishuddha), which could be the throat, provides the verbal communication for ours and fact.

The sixth (Ajna), lives in the third and keeps our intuition.

The crown of heaven is home to the Sahaswara seventh (or Sahaswara) which is the 1000 petal lotus. It can lead to spiritual connection, and enlightenment of ourselves and others.

Meditation can help you heal your Chakras

These steps will help you to learn how to meditate on chakras in order balance and arrange your energy.

1.Chakra meditation involves laying down in a comfortable position with your spine straight. However, it should not be ridged.

You will then need to start focusing on one part of the body starting at the feet and going up. As you do this, let your stress melt away and allow the body to relax.

2. Now, you need to concentrate on your inhalation. Allow your breathing to slow down and become steady. The brain will be confused. Simply bring the attention back to the breath. The oxygen is entering the lungs through the inhalation and going into the blood stream. It will nourish all of your cells, muscles, and organs. Next you will see it purifying the harmful toxins in your body that you exhale with every breath.

3. Next, use chakra deep breathing to visualize the beat of the center and the ideal aspect of the entire body. You will discover how all parts are connected in harmony. These components, as well as the entire body, are sustained by the

breath. You must be aware that the body's life-giving force is the breath.

4. Next, picture a life of power. This is what chakra meditation looks like. This power can be described as a yellowish orange color. This energy covers your entire body and infuses the aura your. As this energy is infused into the aura your, imagine the aura getting brighter, lighter, and charged with this incredible power. Keep doing this steady, let the aura grow brighter slowly and keep this energy moving in with each breathe.

5. The next thing that we want to do with chakra meditation, is to energize each individual chakra. Start by starting at the lowest point of your spine with the root. Imagine a clockwise swirling electricity. The power you breathe in, as well as the electricity it produces, feeds this particular swirl. It becomes brighter and more powerful. Let's imagine that another

source of power is coming from the earth. This is the exact same source of energy, which contributes to the swirling electricity at the root chakra.

6. Next in chakra deep breath, we would like the sacral to be moved as much as the sun plex chakra. Next, we want to move as much as the sacral chakra in chakra deep breathing. You can take your time and not worry about how much you spend on one chakra. It's strongly advised to always work your way up from the bottom. Each chakra will influence the other chakras. Energizing a higher chakra than a lower chakra may have an adverse effect.

7.The final stage of chakra mediation is to imagine all of your chakras becoming a feed by the power flowing out of your breathing and up from planet. The life-giving energy makes you super brighter and clearer by seeing the chakras.

8. We can finally open our eyes and let our minds relax for a few more minutes. Take a look at your body and see how much more energized and relaxed you feel. Do 15-30 minutes of meditation each day. This is an uplifting and enjoyable chakra meditation.

Seven Powerful Ways to Heal the Chakras

These 7 powerful strategies can help you heal any one, two, or all 7 chakras.

CHAKRA Relief Key #1: Flower ESSENCES

A floral essence is vibrational treatment. It can be placed under the tongue or in liquid to provide a subtly but powerfully stimulating effect. Although they may look similar to aromatherapy oils and have a strong scent, floral essences are not. Instead, they contain the therapeutic vibrations of a bloom preserved in water, brandy, and are completely unscented. They can be found at most health food shops. This is where you may be thinking about the next flower essence treatments for each chakra.

Pine is the Root Chakra

Sacral Chakra: Crabapple

Solar Plexus Chakra: Mustard

Holly: Heart Chakra

Honeysuckle for the throat chakra

Star of Bethlehem - Third Eye Chakra

Crown Chakra Wild Rose

CHAKRA Therapy Key #2: Crystals Crystals Crystals make great friends when it comes to changing imbalances in chakras. Crystals are like flower essences. They also work on the vibrational levels to bring about positive changes. Here you'll find useful crystals for each chakra. Clean the crystal healing crystal or crystal jewelry after you receive it. Place the crystal on top of the chakra to receive healing. Relax, take a deep breath, and allow your energy to shift.

Garnet: Root Chakra

Sacral Chakra: Citrine Quartz

Solar Plexus Chakra: Yellow Topaz

Aventurine is a heart chakra

Aquamarine: Throat Chakra

Third Eye Chakra, Sodalite

Crown Chakra Spirit Quartz

CHAKRA #3: AROMATHERAPY

Aromatherapy has a positive impact on our mind, bodies and souls. A diffuser or oil burner can be used to diffuse the essential oils. This will help with chakra healing.

Root Chakra - Patchouli or Vetiver

Sacral Chakra: Ylang Ylang

Solar Plexus Chakra Tangerine

Roses for the Heart Chakra

Clary Sage is the Throat Chakra

Peppermint for the Third Eye Chakra

Crown Chakra - Lavender

CHAKRA #4: VISUALIZATION

Visualization allows you to channel your mind's energy towards positive change. Imagine yourself wrapped up in bright, shining light while you breathe deeply. White light is good for balancing other chakras. However, you can imagine the brightness in the color of the chakra that you wish to heal. It is also possible to use guided chakra clearing visualizations, especially if it is performed on a regular basis.

CHAKRA Healing Key #5: A Sea salt BATH

Warm salt water combined with sea salt can detoxify both the energy field as also the body. Use warm water to dissolve 1 cup of salt. A white-colored candle can be lit and soaked for 20 minutes.

CHAKRA #6 Healing Key: White SAGE

You can quickly get a general power boost by inhaling the smoke from a dried bundle of white sage. A bundle of dried out white Sage should be lit and used as incense. You will want to place some of the burning embers onto a plate or dish. Next, you can move the sage around the energy field so that the smoke is absorbed. After you have managed to extinguish it, either by placing it in water or sealing it in an empty mason jar.

CHAKRA Healing Schlüssel #7: A SELENITE WOMAN

A selenite-wand can be used as a general detoxifier and energy balancer. It won't go off like white colored sage. Use it to balance the energy fields of a foot or other area of the body, and pay particular attention to any chakra parts that you are trying to heal.

Chapter 8: Crown Chakra

This chakra is pure and higher consciousness. This illusion has been stripped away, and it is now crystal clear to you that You are One and One is You. This is the highest point of ascension of kundalini. Once she reaches it, the illusions of duality are wiped away. You are no longer a separate entity, but a part of the larger Universe. It is one existence.

The symbol of this chakra, a thousand-petal lotus, is its symbol. Some images show this lotus pure white while others display it with many different colors. Most images show the lotus with 50 petals in each row, and 20 total. It is depicted on top of the head as a crown. This is only the major chakra that reaches beyond the body and into the Universe. It is linked to both the body and the Universe in equal measure. The chakras all work together to help you focus.

This is Kundalini's most difficult awakening. It is your chakra for transcendence and enlightenment. Uranus is the planet associated with this chakra. It is not linked with the pituitary.

Shri Lalita Devi is Shri Lalita Devi. This goddess is called "thousand-named" and supports the symbolic image of a 1,000-petal lotus. Shri Lalita Devi is a supporter of awakening and rising kundalini inside yourself. She also helps others awaken kundalini.

Some refer to enlightenment as "rebirth", which is the pinnacle kundalini-spiritual awakening. This is where you can become one, and no longer be attached to your body. It is difficult to grasp and accept the significance of this chakra's awakening. It is difficult for most humans to grasp the significance and function of this connection.

Imagine the Universe's vibration as a wonderful chorus or orchestra. It combines and blends in harmony. Before this, you could only hear your own vibration. But now you are simply listening. You weren't actively participating in the sounds. You now have your unique vibration.

Mixes with the Universe's melody, you will join the eternal "song".

You can feel disconnected with your Higher Power if your Crown is not balanced. It's possible to doubt your faith in God and beliefs. Sometimes you can feel down and sad. It's common to feel sad and down. The Universe's purpose is revealed to you when your Crown reawakens.

Meditation to Awaken the Crown Chakra

To open and awaken the Crown chakra, use this guided meditation.

1. Relax in a comfortable seated position with straight shoulders and a straight back. While you are able to relax into your seat, keep your spine straight. Allow your jaw, neck and shoulders to relax. Place your hands on the ground and close your eyes. Your hands should be positioned over your Solar Plexus. Lay your left thumb down on your Sternum. Then, layer your right thumb onto top. Interlace all of your fingers, excluding your pinkies. Spread your pinkies out from your body.

2. Deeply inhale into your nose. Then exhale completely through your mouth. Breathe in through the nose.

3. Take a deep breath and focus on your Third Eye. Feel your third eye awake and full of energy.

4. Put your mind on your Crown. Visualize your thousand-petal lotus becoming one with the Universe. There is no beginning nor end to the flower.

5. Feel the power and primal energy of kundalini flowing through your Sacral chakra, from your Root around Sushumna to your Sacral chakra. It flows in the water from your Sacral Chakra to your Solar Plexus' fire, before passing through your Heart's sacred breath to reach your Throat. Kundalini is heard in the space of your throat before

Filling your Crown and piercing through the illusions of Third Eye. When it fills you Crown, it explodes out into the Universe in the form of a volcanic eruption.

6. You can bring your awareness to your body and watch the kundalini energies rise and fall, flowing freely through your body.

You are continually bringing in energy and pouring it into the Universe.

7. Your Crown chakra awake. It is balanced. Let your attention drift back to the space you are in and the spot you are sitting. Your eyes will open if you close them. Begin to blink slowly as you feel the soothing energy of your Crown.

8. Your body will be more flexible if you roll your neck or shoulders and move your fingers and toes slowly. Continue your day once you're ready.

Yoga to Awaken Your Crown Chakra

Yoga asanas, also known as poses, can be used to improve your physical health and awaken your chakras. Begin by warming up before trying the poses. Do some good stretches, or do a few Sun Salutations before you start to move into the poses.

1. You can also call it "Savasana," or corpse pose. Lay down flat on your back, with your feet extended in front. Keep your arms straight out in front of you. To support your neck, place your chin in front of your chest. Next, pull your shoulder blades backwards. This position is easy to maintain. You can move your shoulders around until you find a spot that you are comfortable with. As your eyes close, visualize a purple haze around your body that emanates from your Crown. The purple will appear as a pulse. Each pulsation emits more of its effect. Continue to breathe deeply, and you can rest up to 15 minutes in this position. It is connected to the Crown and gives you the feeling of being full.

awakened kundalini.

2. Half Lotus pose (or "Ardha Padmasana") is a seated posture that involves crossing your legs in front. You will stack one leg on

top the other. Align the top of your shin with that of your lower shin. Also, align the top foot with your lower foot. If this is uncomfortable, rest one leg on the other's thigh and the other on the top shin. Next, tuck your second foot under your first side's thigh, so you are cross-legged. Place both your knees on the ground and adjust your feet as needed. This will help you find the Earth's support. Your spine should be straightened and extended by taking a deep, exhaling. You can rest your arms in prayer, or on your knees. While you focus on the awakening and kundalini of the Crown, close your eyes. You can stay in this position for as long as you like, but you may move whenever you feel like it. Switch legs and place the bottom leg on the top of one another. Then, switch sides.

3. Supported Headstand pose or "Salamba Sirhasana" - Start on all fours and lower your forearms to touch the ground. You

can turn your palms in front of you and interlace your fingers. Your elbows will be pinned to the Earth, and under your shoulders. Drop your Crown down to the Earth between your forearms. You can use your intertwined hands to surround your head. Bring your hips high and balance your body into the air. Then, start walking with your tips-toes closer towards your head and hands. Your Root will be lifted up to the Sky as you begin to shift your weight to your hands. When your body is inverted, bend your knees. Your knees should be bent as you lift your legs straight up. You can now straighten your legs up into the air, and hold this pose for between three and seven breaths. Begin to bend your knees, then drop your toes to the ground. Slowly, roll out of this pose supporting your neck and head as you return to your feet. As long as you are comfortable, your Crown should remain on the mat.

Mantras for Balance Your Crown Chakra

Sit comfortably in a comfortable, seated position. Take a deep inhale. Then slowly repeat.

One of these mantras

"Wahe Guru."

The following is the translation of this mantra:

"I am in ecstasy.

This simple chant describes the process that takes you from ignorance to knowledge to reach light. This simple chant expresses the human emotion of wonder and elation at witnessing this transformation. This mantra is also helpful in balancing the energies of enlightenment. This mantra helps Kundalini avoid the overwhelm that may occur after this chakra has been fully opened. For some practices, the chanting of the mantra "Har," over 11,000 times is equivalent to one-time evoking "Wahe Guru."

"Om."

The following is the translation of this mantra:

"Ultimate consciousness."

This mantra can be used to awaken your Third Eye chakra. It's also effective in awakening your Crown chakra. It's all about how you intend to chant it. It is an excellent way to open your Crown. While it's possible to chant this chant quietly, the power lies with the stimulation caused by the external and internal vibrations. When you are chanting for your Crown and closing your eyes, consider bringing your awareness towards your Crown.

Chapter 9: Science & Philosophy Of The Third Eye

The third eye can be described as our ability or potential to perceive what is possible. Everyone has access the third eye. Only a few can activate it through meditation and other means. It is possible to sense signals and perceive things through your third eye, even if you don't realize it. You may have used your third eye to perceive a hunch, or a feeling of being unable to stand still. This is the most basic form of third eye signals. As such, it's a complex phenomenon. Our third eye symbolises a sense. One that we can make more reliable, refined, effective, and intuitive than a simple "gut feeling" or intuition.

What is the Third Eye, and How Does It Work?

The pineal gland in the third eye is where all of our psychic abilities and intuition are located. It is thought that the third-eye is the source of our sixth sense. This is the "meta" part that allows mind and senses work in unison. It acts as an all-encompassing sensory and power organ. This makes the pineal gland the main point for creating and perceiving visions.

The third eye is believed be a gateway to higher realms. It can also symbolize that same highly enlightened state. The third eye in Eastern and Western spiritual disciplines is known to be either the "inner eyes" or a mysterious/esoteric phenomena. It refers to our Ajna. Predictably, the third-eye is often associated with out of body experiences, premonitions, inexplicable sightings, telepathy and clairvoyance. "Seers" are people who have an exceptionally developed third eye.

Both Buddhism as well as Hinduism refers to the third-eye symbolizing spiritual awakening. It is often called the "eye of insight" or the "eye of knowledge" in the ancient Hindu tradition. There are many references and representations of the third-eye in Indian iconography. They include a dot in middle of forehead or an actual, real eye on forehead of Hindu deities (such Lord Shiva) as well as other enlightened animals. To symbolise the third eye in Hindu traditions, a mark or tilak is visible between the eyebrows.

The pituitary brain and the pineal body are tiny organs found in our brain. Our pineal gland is often called an "atrophied 3rd eye". However, medical science believes that the glands have not been completely lost. These glands were once useful for humans in the past to access their inner lives. Evolution has made it possible for the glands to serve the same purpose once again. The events of evolution have brought about a complete circle. Humans will be able again to use their clairvoyance ability by recalling ways of connecting with the pituitary organ and pineal gland. A much greater scale, humans will also be able to connect their pituitary gland and pineal body with the cerebrospinal network. Once this is possible, the enlightened person will have complete control over their own will.

Meditation is one method that can activate our third eyes. Meditation is an excellent way to activate both the pineal and pituitary glands. This allows you to relax your mind and explore all its possibilities. Once you have achieved this, clairvoyance is easily accessible.

Our third eye's power can be used in many ways. For example, seers can use their third eyes to uncover deeper links between questions or answers. Energy professionals also experience the energy around them, and then use that energy to manipulate it. You use your third eye to sense, experience, and feel the emotions of others when you show empathy. There are many ways that people use the power and insight of their third eye every day.

What is the third eye and how does it work? Let's see how the concept of third eye works. We can use our third eye to "visually" interpret and sense energy vibrations around. You can see everything through the third-eye, including activity and motion. This is in addition to your ability using the five traditional senses to see and to project potential. It allows you to predict what might happen based on the information available. An inner visual map allows you to perceive the flow of energy, motion, activity, and movement. Your perception of energy is expanding to create mental images and predict outcomes, rather than relying on the third or abstract concept of the third eye. It becomes an actual attribute that allows us learn to communicate with and sense people, places, and things on a deeper level.

The indigo-colored third eye of the chakra system is often linked to our third. This chakra, sometimes called the sixth chakra or the avenue to inner knowledge, is often linked to the third eye. The power of third eye allows us to tap into inner wisdom and helps us to put everything we've learned into perspective. We can gain insight and visuals by gradually opening our brow chakra.

The third eye, then, is our spiritual epicenter. It is possible to communicate our wishes and discover aspects of our lives that we have not yet seen. Practitioners who want to cleanse or open their sixth energy chakra or third eyes must also cleanse their hearts. As the majority of energy flowing into the third-eye originates from our hearts, so it is important that they cleanse them. Chakra meditation allows us to clear all energy blocks from our chakras and facilitate the unhindered flow energy to different chakras.

The geometric center of our brain houses the third and final eye. It is located just below the eyes and is connected to the third ventriculare. This connects to several biorhythms that our body often uses. Our hypothalamus and pineal glands work in close collaboration. The gland directs hunger, thirst, sexual desire, as well the patterns of the biological clock that affects our aging. The ability to master the third eye gives you more control over the forces that shape your behavior.

Chapter 10: How To Cope With Unintentional Awakenings

Sometimes the Kundalini activates in spite of a person's intention. You may have a few reasons for this.

* Genetic predisposition

* Near death experiences

* Extreme events

* Childbirth

* Illnesses

* Accidents

* Physical trauma

* Psychological trauma

* Energetic influences on the environment

* Concentration (such is if you are working in a job which requires concentration)

* Supernatural intervention

* Soul contract (the plan to the soul for this life)

* Existing spiritual practices from previous lives

If you do work that requires you to focus for long periods of times, you may be more likely than others to experience awakening symptoms. Kundalini activity benefits from concentration. Kundalini symptoms have increased in recent years due to more focused jobs than the manual labor. Kundalini symptoms are now more widely known so people can report their experiences and share them with others.

Some people consider orgasm a form Kundalini Release. But what happens? The energy flows to the second chakra in the vicinity of the genitals rather than all the way to its crown. Tantric practices promote sexual stimulation to increase energy, but discourage climax to limit the accumulation of energy. Some abstain entirely from all forms of sexual activity.

Root chakra is responsible for surviving life-threatening events. This is when the Kundalini might be activated. Many believe this is why people in danger can do amazing things such as carrying heavy objects or swimming across miles of freezing water. This can be explained by adrenaline. However, it is possible for the Kundalini to be the physical manifestation of this adrenaline rush.

The body may be left if a person's conscious believes it is in mortal peril. This is known to be an out of body encounter (OBE). Kundalini is characterized by experiencing the sensation of being completely detached from one's body and witnessing events as if one were not there. This is normal. Relax and wait until your consciousness returns into its physical container. Try exploring your environment if adventure is what you seek. To keep you company and to guide you through the experience, you may be accompanied perhaps by a spirit guardian.

Be aware that if you have ever done energy work, or any spiritual practice, you might experience symptoms before your Kundalini actually rises. You may notice synchronistic events occurring that will eventually bring about positive changes in your lives. Your inner life could become richer. You might be more attentive to your feelings and thoughts.

It is possible for you to experience changes in your beliefs, or even question some of the things you believe in. These things are part of the "purging", but don't believe that they are signs that you are being slowed down by the Universe. Consider it a challenge that will improve your abilities on many different levels.

An awakened Kundalini might be considered positive but an unanticipated release of Kundalini can sometimes cause discomfort. There are several things you can do if you experience this.

* Relax your entire body

* Breathe in peace

* Visualize the Kundalini's gentle energy as a gentle breeze or wispy Cloud.

* Do not resist or fear your experiences

* Get advice from someone who has already experienced it.

* Don't analyse the event. Just let it happen.

These methods will be covered in detail later in this book. These methods aim to not strain against Kundalini and to stop contributing energy to the Kundalini.

Helpful Attitudes

These are some attitudes you can adopt to help the Kundalini become activated, regardless of whether it is voluntary or not.

* Mindfulness - Paying attention to the external and internal stimuli without thinking about it

* Self-transcendence: People who can let go their personal issues and have mystical experiences are more likely to experience self-transcendence

* Inner Knowledge - Inwardly focusing one's awareness is a key component of meditation

* Inner calm: Turbulent emotions or preoccupations can prevent Kundalini from manifesting.

* Non-resistance – To facilitate Kundalini flowing more easily, it's better just to be with it than to try to stop it.

* Follow the instructions - Kundalini teachers are responsible for ensuring that Kundalini students adhere to all instructions. It is possible for students to be injured or lose their awakening.

A note about compliance: A guru is someone who you have to follow without question. This is common among Hindus as it is expected in their culture. Hindu literature advises that people choose gurus without discrimination. Find one you trust enough to believe in, and then you can put your faith in them.

Trust is crucial because it helps to establish a good relationship and allows the subtle energies of both you and your guru to flow more harmoniously. Your negative feelings can become more intense if your guru is doubtful. Kundalini also increases your sensitivity. Relaxing and trusting in your teacher can reduce stress.

The Kundalini will be activated until it wakes up. But, Kundalini will continue to activate if you maintain your energy so it doesn't become blocked. Enlightenment is an ongoing process. Because many things in life can lower your vibratory level, it may be necessary to repeatedly clear and awaken. The rest of the book will address clearing and maintaining the health of your energetic body.

Remember that Kundalini awakening signs can also be caused by normal everyday things. You should always have your body checked to make sure there are no health problems. If you believe the symptoms might be psychological, see a mental healthcare professional. So that you don't create more problems, make sure you don't mix physical and mental issues with energetic/spiritual.

If you suspect that Kundalini has been prematurely awakened, you should talk to a Guru about it. The guru will be able determine if you have it. If you don't have one, you might try your luck at clairvoyants or energy workers. They will help you understand what is going on and how to cope.

It's important that you rule out all possible causes of the symptoms. You shouldn't assume that your Kundalini awakening is paranormal. Failure to do this can lead to psychiatric or medical problems. While it might be tempting to believe the strange symptoms you are seeing are Kundalini manifestations. However, if they aren't, you risk putting yourself at risk. Make sure you take care of yourself first. Healthy body and mind are the best foundation for amplifying your spirit.

These can generally be divided into methods in which the disciple is able to awaken his/her energy on her/his own or those where a mentor wakes up the energy. It is more convenient to have a Guru do the awakening. However, enlightened Gurus are not common.

Prepare to Wake Up

Here's how to get your torpid Kundalini energy going to make the most out of its numerous benefits. This isn't directed reflection but a highly engaged method for activating Kundalini in your body.

1. Relax your body fully and inhale slowly to allow for relaxation. Make sure you're wearing comfortable clothes, and that you're in a quiet space with no interruptions. Gradually close the eyes.

2. Use delicate stomach breathing techniques. See the oxygen entering your throat and lungs. This is the easiest

approach to recognize the secret energy path.

The moment we inhale, the growing lungs reach the midsection (stomach), and then the pelvic organs.

3. Allow your lungs and stomach to achieve harmony, by gently moving together.

4. Identify your kidneys. These kidneys are located behind the film that is between the airbags in your stomach and lungs. With every inward breathe, attach your kidneys and discharge both airbags. This could end up rubbing your kidneys. Avoid opening your eyes.

5. Keep an eye on the area where your adrenal organs are located near the kidneys. Start reciting "Num Mum Yum Pa'Hum." Begin to let your sacks touch each other as you breathe in. Recite the words and then breathe out. Bring the

present second into your body to feel unity.

6. Rub your lower back and ribs using your rear end with both of your palms. Avoid sitting in an unbending posture and eliminate all inconveniences.

7. Lift your arms up above your head and stretch your thumbs out. Be deliberate about how your lungs responds to signals received through the thumbs. As you raise your forefinger towards heaven, allow the internal organ of your ribcage to dangle from it.

8. Your collarbones should be raised. Stretch out from your collarbones to reach your hanging kidneys. Then, follow it by pivoting and squeezing each one of your feet. Attract your attention again to the two inflatable bags. Enjoy the sensations of the two airbags along with the middle and adrenal.

9. Begin to empty your stomach. However, don't exhale everything at once. Simply open your jaw slightly, and you will be able to make a delicate situation in your throat. It will assist with moderate exhalation.

10. As you inhale, touch the two sacks on your stomach and lungs, while resting your taste, jaw, and tongue over the spinal pile.

11. Slowly take a deep breath in, and then slowly exhale. With each inhalation imagine creating wings and imagining the wings reaching out to the top of your lungs.

12. Inhale deeply and connect the pleural pouch pack to your pelvis and sack of midregion. You can breathe out slowly and allow the third (spinal, dural) pack above your nose.

13. Allow your dural sack to grow underneath your arch. Allow the spinal string to ascend from the spine. Find the

secret pathway to the focal energy channel and start your hunt.

14. Find the energy vibration at the base of your spine. While keeping your eyes shut, serenade "Vacuum, Vacuum, Vacuum, Vacuum." This will enable you to have more flexibility and capacity. This will make your spine feel more solid and flexible. Recite "Vacuum" to feel the vibration rising up your spine.

15. Consider yourself an instrument that spreads delight. You are an instrument to spread joy. Each bearing conveys affection, empathy, thoughtfulness, and compassion.

16. Chant "Shum-shumshumshumshum" The sacrum bone will vibrate with the sound of this serenade. Look out for the craniosacral vibration that begins to rise from the spine.

Feel the third sack, which is filled with liquid flooding and then slowly settling down. Allow your mind sink into that water. Allow it to glide slowly.

17. Imagine an inflatable twice as big as the pelvis and mid-region. You can slowly release the air from the inflatable by holding its mouth and slowly extending it. This will allow you point the little airfly anywhere you want.

18. You can lift your pelvic area marginally, and then crush your buttcentric muscles enough to see or visualize a ring. These muscles control the flow of air that you inhale. You can allow the two bags to come in contact by gently inhaling. The kidneys can be compared between the two airbags. Allow the jaws to rest over the air.

19. Move the third mindsack marginally forward, while raising your spinal line

gradually. You can now raise your pelvic floors, connect with the rings of your spinal base and breathe out slowly.

20. Now, blow the stomach stream in the opposite direction from the front-facing empty on your upper sacrum down to the lower spine. Look for the secret area to the focal energy channel. The secret section is located in your lower back, midsection catch, and inner areas of your stomach. You will feel a tingling sensation in your stomach if you place your palms on both sides.

21. Push in and create a total exhalation channel within the focal energy channels. If you suspect you have initiated a hidden hook, or you are unsure of your vulnerability, lift your head and keep your eyes closed. In the event that you are confronted with one, push through it. You should pass by any street you find. Keep

gazing upward. Breathe in. After that, you can rest your sacks.

22. Engage your pelvic muscles. Breathe out again from your left side, towards your midline which is located under the navel. Rehearse it several times. Serenade "Bum Ba'Hum Mum Yum Rum Lum." These are sounds that correspond to six petals in the Svadhisthana lotsus chakra. Moving from the right lower middle-region to your supplement to right kidney, then to one side kidney, left col, and lastly the left ovary.

23. Chant "Lum LumLumLumLumLum," to ask for the beauty and all-inclusive abilities or all-powerful. Breathe in towards the focal line by breathing out to the left. Allow the three bags to rest.

24. The spine is the best place to bring your mindfulness down. While you are breathing in, make the sound "H" and

allow your lower stomach area to expand rapidly. Imagine flipping hotcakes or bread. Breathe in forward, and let it circle with the little fly before the midregion division divider. It then passes through the divider to reach the spinal section's fore-facing space. If you feel troublesome, continue to inhale slowly and gently, working towards your final objective of harmony.

Chapter 11: How You Can Develop And Use The Psychic Senses

Have you ever thought you could develop psychic abilities or had psychic senses? Although it is possible to improve your psychic abilities there are some challenges. This chapter will examine the various ways that you can harness intuition and make it work for your best.

You should commit to practicing these techniques daily. There is no specific order of exercises you should do. However, the only rule is to put it into practice.

You can choose from the list below which one resonates most with you, and which is FUN. Keep at it for as long as you can before moving onto the next. The ability to tap into your psychic abilities takes effort and time.

1- Meditating is key

Your vibration should be increased if you are to develop psychic abilities. The higher frequency required for this spirit chakra vibrates at a higher rate. Meditation will allow you to relax, be more in touch with your energy vibration and become more intuitive. Meditation will help you connect with Spirit, the Higher Self, as well as energy that radiates out of another person.

2- Seeking guidance from your spirit

Talk up and let your Spirit Guides be more visible while you are in meditation. Trust your meditations, keep an open mind, and connect to these guides so that they can be heard even when you are not in meditative.

3- Practicing psychometry

Psychometry of things is one part of harnessing your psychic powers. Understanding and practicing it is an essential part of this process. Psychometry refers the ability to detect energy that is emanating from something, someone or an object. This is an excellent way to get started with your psychic abilities. Just hold an object. Now, take the object in your hands and close your eyes to test whether you can sense or hear any information about it.

4- Using Zener cards

Zener cards can also be shared with a friend to improve your mental capabilities and outreach. A friend can help you choose a card and then they can look through it together. You can then attempt to communicate this image to them without ever speaking or showing the card.

5-Start with flower visualization

Flower visualization is a great way to start your psychic ability. You can develop your psychic abilities, including clairvoyance. This exercise can be done with a simple bouquet or a collection of flowers you have in your yard. Now, take some time to examine the flowers. Next, close you eyes slowly and try to imagine one of each flower from the bundle. The next step is to visualize the flower in vivid detail in your mind.

6- Develop your clairvoyance using random visualization

You must have practiced flower visualization before you can do this activity. With your eyes closed, relax and get into an easy position. Your third eye should be your focus. Next, ask the spirit guides for images that are peaceful and beautiful. Allow yourself to be guided by the spirit, not your thoughts. Allow your mind space to wander, and let the images flow into third eye.

7- Walking with nature

It doesn't matter if it's in nature, or with nature. It doesn't matter if meditation is boring. Meditation can be done at any place, anytime and from any position as long you're in a safe and comfortable environment. The ability to be in tune with the natural world enhances your awareness. It doesn't matter whether you are standing, sitting or walking. Just focus on you and your breath. You can clear your mind by exhaling and inhaling. This will increase your vibrations and help you to feel more positive.

8- Reading

Reading helps you not only understand your psychic abilities, senses, and how they work, but also prepares you for life and the changes taking place in your own mind. Reading books can help you to connect with your divine support network and activate your Kundalini. You can also subscribe to posts from mediums and psychics around the world. Stay informed with the latest news in spirit and psychic realms.

9- Visiting Antique stores

Is there ever a feeling that you have an instinctive sense of when you are in antique shops? Do you find it annoying? Check out the store for an object that you can sense. Do you hear a name? Get a vision? These activities will help you develop your psychic abilities.

11- Keep your symbol book

As you work towards developing and enhancing your psychic skills, it is more likely that you will come in contact with psychic information or be able to see it in different ways. These often come in the form symbols that should not be taken too literally. This information will be easier to interpret if you trust your spirit guides. Keep these symbols in your symbol book. This will make a great keepsake over the years.

12- Make a tarot deck.

You might be using a Tarot deck, and if so, you should also keep a tarot guide. The design and feel of the deck are important to you. To decode the meanings of the tarot, you can use the guide provided with the deck to guide you. You can meditate every day and spend some time with each card. Once you are done, you can write down your thoughts about the cards and their meanings in your tarot books. This is an excellent way to improve your psychic abilities.

13- Practice seeing auras

Aura reading and sighting is quite simple. Some people are naturally good at reading auras, while others need to be taught. It is also a great way to improve your psychic skills. To begin, ask a friend or family member to stand before a wall. Take a step back, about eight feet. Now focus your attention towards the forehead of your friend. Think of looking through your friend at the wall behind them. If you practice this frequently, sooner you will start to notice the aura layer that surrounds your friend.

14- Developing your clairaudience

Clairaudience also means psychic hearing. Every night before going to sleep, lie quietly in bed, your eyes closed. Pay attention to what you hear around. This may be difficult if your home is in a busy city. However, you can train your ears to focus on what you hear. Your intuition will improve if you pay attention to the sounds that are often ignored.

15- Take readings often

It is crucial to be a psychic by giving readings. If you have all the knowledge about football but do not play football, then you will never be a professional footballer. This is the same thing as developing your psychic ability.

16- Turning your pet in

Pets and domestic animals are able to sense their intuition. You can calmly observe your pet when it is calm and then try to empathize with their emotions. This will build a stronger relationship between you, your pet, and also allow you to develop clairsentience.

17- Reading old family photos

Reading family photos is one of the most fun ways to enhance and practice your psychic abilities. You can look at black-and white photos of family members that you have never seen and gaze into the eyes of the people. Write down your feelings and impressions when you see these photos. You'll discover something new each time you view the photos at different times.

18- Keep a journal

Writing down your thoughts and feelings in a journal is a good way to connect with your Higherself. When you feel the need for guidance, keep it in your journal. This will help to relax and allow your divine guide to help you.

19- Pray

Praying can make you feel more connected, love, and supported by God.

20- Connect Telepathically

To make it work, this must be practiced often. Do you often say, "I have been thinking about your and it just so happened that you called!"? This could be you calling your friend via telepathic communication.

21- Join a spiritual development class

These classes will help you not only learn about your psychic abilities but also give you a safe and loving place to connect with your abilities and senses.

22- Get to know other mediums, psychics

In previous chapters, we have talked about the importance of surrounding yourself with like-minded persons who can help you reach your goals. You can channel your psychic abilities in the same way. You will learn more and receive help if you seek the support of people with knowledge and experience.

23. Turning your gifts ON

You should learn how to control psychic abilities and psychic senses as soon you develop them. This means that your psychic abilities are not always on, and you do not pick up vibes or auras from anyone around you. Your support circle is essential. It is important to learn how to open your psychic communication so that you can turn your gifts ON only when they are needed.

24- Turn them OFF!

It is important to switch off any thing that is not working. Once you're done with practicing, you can switch off your abilities.

25- Keeping your eyes on the third Eye

It is important to understand and focus your attention on the third-eye to achieve clairvoyance, one of the most powerful psychic abilities. Imagine this area opening up. With practice, you may even begin to feel the tingling in your third eye.

26- Keep your vibration high

For psychic development, you need to vibrate at high frequencies. Because spirit vibrates at very high frequencies, Being authentic will help you connect with your Higher Self aswell as the Divine. You are more likely to attract spiritual, beautiful people to your life.

27- Eating right

You can also make a high vibration by what you eat. Consuming high vibration food like fruits and veggies will help you feel great, make your body feel great and allow you to develop psychic abilities.

28- Keep an open dream journal

While there may seem to be a lot of journals on the internet, it is essential that you keep only one book. Once you have categorized them, you can then categorize them as meanings, symbols, or dreams. As you increase your psychic abilities, vivid dreams will become more common. This is why it is so important to keep track of them. Our logical minds can often second guess these dreams when we awaken. A dream journal is a great tool in these situations.

Chapter 12: Kundalini Yoga

Kundalini Yoga is a form of Kundalini Yoga that Yogi Bhajan introduced to the Western World in 1968. How can Kundalini yoga be integrated into your daily life? There are many studios available to assist you on your journey towards Kundalini awakening. Your goal is to achieve complete enlightenment, by realigning all your chakras. This energy will often be represented by a snack coiled at your spine. Kriyas, or Kundalini Yoga sequences, are what you will be learning through Kundalini Yoga.

Kriyas

Kriya can also be translated as action. Kundalini Yoga's actions will show you how to translate your intentions into action. As you practice yoga, your body will be guided by sounds, breath, and postures that can help you achieve your goals. Your mind, body, spirit, and behavior can all be changed by physical and mental adjustments. Kriyas help you to balance your liver and your flexibility. Kriya will ultimately affect your entire being.

Kriya is a combination of a number of concepts. First, you have the angles and triangles for asanas. There's also the prana (breath), the repetition and the focus of the mantra. Your session may leave you feeling different. You can adjust your mental preparations for the Kundalini Awakening by practicing meditation or yoga.

It doesn't matter if you want to join a group of practitioners or go it alone, you need to be prepared. We will provide some tips and tricks to help you get started with your Kundalini practice. This will allow you to be prepared before starting your Kundalini journey.

Before Kundalini Yoga

1. To avoid distraction, you should turn off your phone

2. A light snack can be eaten between two and three hours before your session to satisfy hunger.

3. Make sure you wear comfortable clothing, and a natural fiber head covering

4. Comfortable sitting on a blanket made from natural fibers or sheepskin is a good choice. Also, a shawl will be useful to cover you during meditation.

5. You should ensure that water is kept in a sealed container to keep you hydrated

6. A cushion or pillow is a good option if you have limited mobility. So you can be elevated while sitting or lying down, and you can meditate.

7. You don't want to use the Adi Mantra before you start your Kundalini Yoga class. This is "Ong Namoguru Dev Namo." Once you're done, you can begin your practice.

During Kundalini Yoga

1. When you're doing the postures, listen to your body. It is up to you to decide what works best for your body.

2. Make sure you follow all instructions. It is important to maintain the correct posture at all times. Beginners may find it helpful to speed up the exercise.

3. Be sure to keep hydrated

4. Do not limit yourself to what you believe is possible. It's okay to start slowly. But, try to push yourself beyond what you think is possible.

5. If you're a woman, it is important to listen to your body. Yoga is not recommended for the first three day of

your period. Avoid stretching poses such as camel pose or satkriya. Instead, imagine yourself in the posture. If you have any concerns about doing this pose, your teacher can help you modify it.

6. Don't be afraid, if in doubt, to voice your confusion. It is okay to need clarification on a pose.

After Kundalini Yoga

1. The number one rule after yoga is to drink plenty of water. You have just worked your mind, so make sure you nourish your body.

2. Your experience may make you feel different. You might feel different after your session.

3. Make every effort to incorporate the class in your daily life. It is simple to start something. But, sticking with it can prove difficult.

Chapter 13: Power And Benefits Of An Open Third Eye

It is not easy to open your third eye. This will require a lot of concentration and focus. The power of the third-eye can be harnessed by anyone. Anyone can experience the positive changes it can make in their lives. It is not possible for everyone to get motivated to work towards this goal. To open the third eye, you need to persevere and take your time. This section will help explain what you are seeing when you open the third eyes to get a better idea of what you are trying to achieve.

You open your mind and accept the possibilities around you

Principles like the law o f attraction emphasize the importance of energy and how it affects your life. Your third eye will allow you to see the world differently. Instead of seeing what is blocking your path, you will be able to identify and recognize the patterns that can lead you to the future.

Limiting one's options is one of many reasons why people fail to succeed or do not get the life they want. You might be afraid of certain situations, or unsure what steps to take to get there. The power of the third eyes allows you to access the potential in the world. Your soul doesn't need to be asleep; it is available to assist your active mind in realizing your most grandiose desires.

You are free to form your own opinion

Is it possible to meet someone who will not change their mind despite all the facts? This is when people get obsessed with being right. They will accept the most popular view and deny any other. This is how many people turn their backs on the inequalities, injustices, and cruelty in the world.

When you open your third eye, you'll find that you think differently. The critical thinking you develop will make it easier to evaluate and ask questions before you form an opinion or take a final decision.

Your Spirit Awakens

Did you ever hear the term sheeple? This term refers to people who blindly obey, whether it is politics, religion, or another topic. They are not critical thinkers, but simply do what is expected. The world around us becomes more real when your third eye is open. Be prepared to be disappointed if you find the world dark. The world is full of powerful figures who work other people like puppets. Everywhere you look, there are injustices and inequalities. As you learn more about the world, you will also discover beautiful places. The third eye will open and change your motivations. It will allow you to move toward a more accessible lifestyle that allows you to experience greater compassion, truth, and love.

You'll get better sleep

Pineal gland functions include controlling sleep and wake cycles. You will feel more rested if you open your third eyes. Many people also experience vivid dreams. The possibilities are endless, and you will soon realize how unlimited the realm of dreams truly is. As you discover the immense potential of your spiritual selves, the possibilities will only continue to grow.

There are many ways to experience astral travel

Some people learn astral travel by accessing the third eye. Once you understand that there is no limit to what you can do, you will realize that your physical existence does not define you. Unless you allow them to dominate you, time and space are not fixed elements that you can rely on. Some people describe this as their soul's ability to leave their body and travel to any location in the universe.

You will develop a deeper intuition

Some people have a strong sense of intuition when they open their third eye. This phenomenon is commonly called a sixth or sixth sense. Some people have psychic abilities deep in their bones. These abilities can be tapped into the instinctual information being sent by the world. This goes a long ways in explaining the proverbial "all you have to know is inside." By expanding your consciousness, and turning your attention inward, you can discover the secrets of this world.

You will have a greater understanding of your needs and desires.

It is very easy to get distracted from the material pull in the world. Advertisements are everywhere. They tell us what we need to feel happy. Many people view success as making the most money possible, and even more money in a lifetime. This leads to many people feeling unhappy, uncertain about what goals they should pursue to fulfill the promise of "dreams".

The world's material needs and desires will not be as important when your third eye opens. You will be able to see what makes you happy and what the best path is for you to reach it.

You'll Feel More Creativity

People who feel restricted by the physical world they live in often find it difficult to accept the judgements and guidelines of others. People often feel like others are criticizing their creativity, since it cannot be controlled or mandated. If you can open the third eye, the boundaries of the world around your are broken. You feel empowered to tackle your creative projects and make them real.

Stress Will Melt away

Awakening your third eye changes the way you feel about the world. It makes it less significant. A reduced stress level and anxiety can help you see that all the little things in the world matter less in the big picture. It gives you more control over the stressors in your life and allows you the opportunity to make a bigger, more positive impact on your own life.

The third eye gives insight into how to make stress melt away. Instead of focusing your attention on the stress and anxiety you feel, you will discover that your mind is open for solutions. Each day you will wake up determined to reach your goals and get rid of the stressors in your life.

Greater Quality of Life

The bottom line is that if your third eye is awakened you will be able to attract all the things you need to succeed in your life. You can gain insight into your goals, achieve happiness, and reduce stress. You will feel more connected to yourself and others, have better sleep, be more creative, and may even experience powers such as foresight, astral projection, and seeing auras. All of these factors will work together to improve your quality life so you can live the life you always dreamed.

Chapter 14: Mind Power

Ind power is among your most powerful and helpful abilities.

You can use your imagination and this energy to create success, failure, happiness, opportunities, obstacles, or challenges. All of this will depend on how you think.

Your thoughts are the first component of your power. When you add emotion and focus to them, your thoughts become powerful and can make a difference in the world.

Your thoughts can have a significant impact on your life.

Only some ideas can be equal. Some ideas are more powerful than others.

As thoughts are, so life. Though sensitive thoughts seldom have an effect, thoughts that can be powerful are capable of creating great change.

Mind power refers to your attention, mental images, and thoughts.

Thoughts are energy. Though invisible and subtle they can influence reality.

Your thoughts and mind are as powerful as the wind.

Thoughts' energy is an innovative power. Thoughts play on your mind like a video. The life type that you choose to live is determined by the experiences and thoughts you have.

Play another video to make improvements in your life.

This power is both transferable and can be used for teaching as well as strengthening. It is possible to use it to effect positive change in your life.

Planting seeds is a good idea. Water them and give them fertilizers to help them grow.

Thoughts are seeds. They naturally have the inclination to grow, develop, and be powerful if they are given the right attention and allowed to flourish.

Their effectiveness is determined by their enthusiasm, passion, and attention. A thought that isn't interesting to you will not gain strength and won't be as powerful if it doesn't interest you enough.

Your thoughts are what influence your subconscious, which in turn influences the actions that you take.

Your thoughts could also reach other minds and be affected by them.

You will attract people to your life who are interested in helping you reach your dreams if you focus on your goals.

Powerful thoughts will have an impact on the quality of your life as well as the lives of others. Be skeptical of what your beliefs may lead to.

This may seem strange and outlandish. This does not mean you need to understand these words. But if you take a look at your beliefs and the way you live, you will discover amazing things. There is a correlation among one's beliefs and one's life problems.

A Discussion on The Energy of the Mind

We pay little attention to the thoughts of others. They come, pass through our heads and are never to return. Thoughts are also immaterial. We often forget that they are very important. We underestimate how powerful feelings can be on our lives. The human brain still has an incredible potential. It can have some of our strongest abilities. Unfortunately, most of its abilities are undiscovered or ignored, and many have fallen asleep. The brain's ability to use its power is one the greatest. This article will cover the extraordinary energy of your brain and the many things you can accomplish with it.

Your thoughts have the greatest impact on the brain's ability to function. Your beliefs determine what you are. You can often influence what happens in your life by the views you hold. Your attitudes, thoughts and beliefs can have a significant impact on how you behave in certain situations. You can also influence how you view certain situations through your thought patterns. This could have a positive impact.

It is capable of making the big difference between living with a horrible, apocalyptic world that will punish you and living in a world where you are faced with difficult lessons. While two people might share exactly the same experience they may interpret it in a completely different way.

How to Increase Your Mind Power

Your mind power will grow if you learn any one or all of the following techniques.

* Brain Teasers & Games

* Speed Reading

* People Observation

* Meditation

* Critical & Lateral Thinking

* Deeply thinking and wondering

* Writing

* Learn a new language

* Recognizing the Limits of Your Brain

* Neurolinguistic Programming - NLP

* Thought Management

* Mind Control

This list could go on for as long as your mind expands. Many of the above mentioned relate to each other, including Meditation and Mind Control, Language Learning and Writing, and even Mind Control.

A subset of some meanings is another. Because they can only increase the brain's capacity, they are included in this list.

The brain is made up of the left and the right hemispheres. Each hemisphere handles certain psychological tasks. These methods target both the hemispheres.

Brain teasers and other gaming systems work best in the left hemisphere. Wondering engages the correct hemisphere. Some strategies, like writing that stimulates creativity (right half) or linguistic abilities(left half), are the best.

Introduction of the brain Power Techniques

Let's look briefly at the brain power summary.

Brain Mapping

Brain Mapping is an innovative learning method that uses brain abilities to learn more. Who said that learning was linear?

By using brain maps as you learn, your mind can store the information in to long-term memory. A mind chart doesn't follow a linear pattern. It is not possible to examine it in order. It is a simple pattern that contains key information.

Mind mapping is not an alternative method to the traditional way of learning, but it can be used as a supplement. It's an addition analysis tool.

If you have never used mind mapping before, you might want to do so. It is a useful tool that can enhance learning capabilities.

Brain teasers and games Brain teasers are both entertaining, and you can benefit from them as well.

You'll find many kinds of brain games as well as brain teasers. Each type is designed to improve one specific part of the brain. Many mental tasks can be associated with brain areas like the temporal, frontal and parietal. These areas are associated with faster thinking and better performance.

For your brain to stay healthy, it doesn't take you more than fifteen minutes per day.

They describe the brain as a "muscle". You have been training it often. Utilizing your existing neuronal networks is crucial. Simply because if they don't work, then your brain will stop using them. In the end, your entire brain power decreases.

Pace Reading

Speed reading techniques enable you to read more quickly. The difficult part is often to get used. They are sometimes tiring after a while.

Your comprehension decreases if you are able to read more quickly. A system that allows you to read 20000 words per hour at 100 percent comprehension is likely to be a fraud. Keep your money safe.

Individuals Observation

This phrase is my favorite for watching people's reactions, movements, and behavior. Body language is an integral part of this. Individuals Observation goes beyond body language. You also get to observe their mentality as a whole.

You can find commonalities in the way people think in different situations. When you do this subconsciously with everyone you meet, it will become second nature.

At the end you will be able to see the thoughts of others and their emotions. Emotionally charged Intelligence is both developed and improves.

Your ability to observe people, even strangers, improves your psychological skills. You will be able identify possible, malicious intentions, and lies of others.

This was what I did when I first met someone. I would simply observe the people around me, even if there were no one to meet.

This ability finally started to work forever and I rarely do it intentionally anymore. This ability allows me to benefit from interpersonal relationships. It is a great way of getting to know people better and communicating with them more effectively

Critical and lateral Thinking

Lateral Thinking

Critical thinking is generally defined as the ability and skill to critically evaluate a situation, then determine whether you agree or disagree. This situation can be an argument.

Critical thinking, which is left hemisphere oriented, involves essentially reasoning. However, logic is only one product of critical thinking. You also need to have the ability of critical thinking, which includes clarity, fairness and empathy.

There is a widespread belief that those with critical thinking tend not to reject. However, those who mainly reject are not able to think critically. They are afraid of any kind of suspicious behavior.

Lateral thinking is a totally unique way to think. Lateral believing, which is a result of imagination, is a right hemisphere phenomenon. It's also known as "thinking beyond the box".

When you see things from a side view, you can approach problems in an indirect way. You come up with new ideas and perspectives.

Lateral thinking helps you solve problems creatively, and can even lead to solutions that aren't obvious initially. In business and management, lateral thinking is also a valued skill.

Thinking immediately would signify that you're creative and ingenuity would signify that your brain is more powerful.

Deep thinking and deep wondering

Wondering is a sign you have Spiritual Intelligence. Wondering is related with philosophical questions and higher such as the origins of the planet, God's existence, etc.

This type of questions led philosophers and others to express their opinions about the world.

When you have a question, you will often browse the internet to find answers. It's impossible to just draw conclusions about these topics as they remain unsolved.

You'll eventually be satisfied with your explanations and ideas and will see if the planet accepts them.

These processes will open your mind up to a never-ending evaluation of the earth and prompt you to take deep thought.

In our everyday lives, we all have moments for serious thought. Sometimes we discover truths that are not obvious to us, changing our view of the planet.

Compare your current views to those from five years ago. Is it possible to identify topics where you've changed your mind? Even if your practice isn't frequent, it is possible.

Everyday you discover things that will change the way you think. To understand the world and other people around you, you must think deeply.

It's also known as lateral thinking. The ability to see the reasons behind things and to discover how they work can lead you to think sideways. Your consciousness, as well as your mind power, expands when you think deeply.

Writing

Writing is one of these four linguistic skills. The remaining three are reading, listening, or speaking. The posting ability is my favorite because it challenges your imagination and allows you to control the thought for a set time.

The mind can be overwhelmed with ideas and thoughts when creating a publication. It might be difficult to know the best way to begin creating a guide. However, once you do start, your mind is filled with concepts (brainstorming), so you could create for many hours.

Studying another Language

A foreign language can do more to help your mind. Neurogenesis, which is the brain's process of learning a new language or learning it, occurs.

Neurogenesis is a term that describes the creation of new neural networks.

Yet, you can learn new ways to think in another language. Learning new vocabulary, syntax and grammatical rules will enhance your intelligence. It works with all of the subsystems in your brain. It's a comprehensive brainpower technique.

I was previously informed in a magazine that learning new languages slows down the aging process. It is a great way to keep your mind sharp and healthy.

To be able to see your mind's limits

How does this knowledge impact brain expansion? It will keep it you happy and motivated.

This is not a means to an end, but a prerequisite. To reach the goals you need to be able to comprehend your brain's limitations.

Telekinesis can take months or even days to develop. This power is not likely to be created.

The above example illustrates the importance of patience. Setting realistic goals that your mind can achieve will produce better outcomes than setting goals that you lack confidence in.

The brain is not a machine. It is a biological organ. Therefore, it requires sleep. It is important not to force the brain to work 24/7. This will cause it damage. Focus on your brain's needs and you'll lose all your gains.

Also, good brain foods should not be overlooked. They can help increase your brain's potential limit. The brain will reward you for feeding the gray matter well.

The brain needs to sleep. It needs to organize the day's fresh experiences. Give it enough time. You should try to sleep for as long as you need, but not more. Your mind is also not well-suited for oversleeping.

Neurolinguistic Programming - NLP

Neurolinguistic programming is a set of mental techniques that increases your influence more than other people. NLP can improve the way you interact with others.

NLP experts can help you manage people's minds. Although it is hard to achieve this level, you will be able to learn the fundamentals that will help you influence someone.

Believed Management

In this particular chapter I am talking about the ability to manage your head as effectively as setting priorities. This applies to a workplace where multiple tasks need to be completed quickly.

Individuals who are great at concept management can get managerial positions within companies. They could place priorities on a task list and also complete the tasks within the timeframe. You should consider that a job placement like this is very difficult.

To be a strong concept manager skill, you must have the ability to manage yourself well and be calm and relaxed. This is more due to increased brain power than it is because of technique. Controlling stress levels will make it easier to manage the emotions.

Brain Control

Mind control does not just refer to a single practice, but rather a combination of several. Mind control is a category by itself that will raise your consciousness to a higher fitness level. Expect the results to be dramatic and to affect the perception of the entire world.

You will grow your mind by using the tips and techniques discussed here. To level up, you do not have to master every single one. Take it slow and don't worry. You will need patience.

Chapter 15: Throat Chakra

"Vissuddha," which is your Throat, is all you need to communicate.

Here you can express yourself, your truth. It also works in conjunction with your Solar Plexus, your seat of personality and willpower. How you express yourself and your purpose in life is critical to the success of the Universe and your purpose. It would be impossible for the best minds on Earth to have their ideas heard if no one communicated them effectively. All of us have something to share with the world. Share it. The other end of the spectrum has a right for you to be heard.

This chakra has an impact on the throat. It also affects your vocal cords, nose and ears. In order to communicate well you must combine creativity with the ability to hear. Unbalanced listening skills can lead to poor comprehension, misunderstood behavior, gossiping and lying. Your voice might be strong or weak.

If your Throat feels "lumpy", it could be an indication that your Throat might be blocked. By releasing your message, you can "purify" the body. You must clear your block. Crying is a powerful method of communication. Unable to find words or crying out are signs of an unbalanced Throat.

A 16-petaled lotus in light blue is the symbol commonly associated with this chakra. Ether is represented by the symbol of an upside-down triangle with a circle in it. Mercury is the planet that governs the Throat. Sadashiva represents the energy center. They are both males and females and symbolize yin and Yang. Ambara the white elephant is another deity that can be seen using this chakra.

Meditation to Awaken the Throat Chakra

To open and awaken the Throat chakra, use this guided meditation.

1. Relax into a comfortable seated position with straight shoulders and a straight back. Relax into the seat and maintain your balance.

A straight spine is best. Allow your shoulders to relax and your neck to relax. Place your gaze one-foot away from your eyes. With your palms facing down, place your hands on your knees. With your thumb touching your thumb, touch your forefinger with your thumb. Maintain straight arms and a slight bend in the elbow.

2. Deeply inhale into your nose. Then exhale completely through your mouth. Breathe in through the nose.

3. Press the tip end of your tongue to your roof when you exhale. To chant, "Humee Hum Hum Brrahm Hum", you can use your tongue's back to do so.

4. For up to 11 minutes, you can continue this slow-mo chant.

5. You can pay attention to the sound of the chant and the vibrations felt in your neck.

6. Imagine a soft blue light wafting over your vocal cords, breaking down any blocks that may be lodged in your ears and Throat.

7. Your Throat Chakra is awake. It is balanced and flows well. Let your attention drift back to the space you are in and where you're sitting. As if your eyes were closed, open them. You can blink slowly several times, as you take in the energy flowing through your Throat.

8. Your body will be more flexible if you roll your neck, shoulders, and fingers or move your toes slowly. Continue your day once you're ready.

Yoga to Awaken the Throat Chakra

Yoga asanas, also known as poses, can be used to heal your body and awaken your chakras. Make sure you warm up before you try the poses. Do some stretching and Sun Salutations before you start to practice the poses.

You are ready to transform into these poses.

1. "Neck Release." From a comfortable seated position, slowly roll your head around in a circular motion. Do five rotations clockwise, then turn in the opposite directions five times. Turn your chin towards the right when you exhale. Bring your head back to centre. Exhale by bringing your chin back towards the

center. Take a second inhale. Next, move your gaze and chin towards the left. Now exhale. Repeat the motion on each side five times. To inhale, bring your head back to the center. Next, drop your right ear to your right side. You can lift your right arm upwards and rest your hand on your head. This will help you bring your head down to the shoulders. Then inhale to bring it back to the middle. Your left arm should be raised and your left hand placed on your head. This will help to guide the arm toward your shoulder. Repeat the motion on each side five times.

2. Lion Pose (or "Singhasana"): Begin by kneeling, then bring your feet under your head so your heels are in line with your back. You can lengthen your spine by pressing your Crown toward the sky. However, you should keep your seat on your heels. Straighten your arms and place your palms on the floor. Spread your

fingers wide. You can inhale deeply and then open your eyes wide. When you exhale, let out a loud "Haaaaaaaaa!" noise. For five to seven more breaths, repeat this process.

3. Legs up the wall pose, or "Viparitakarani," requires you to sit on your left side, press your right hip against the wall, and then bend your knees so that your feet are flat on the floor. Now, place your legs parallel against the wall. To pivot, lift your legs toward the wall by bringing your Root towards the point where the wall meets your floor. Your knees should not be bent and your legs should press against the wall. Be supportive and keep your arms relaxed. Adjust your position as much or little as you like to create a supportive and relaxed angle. You can take this position for as long as 15 minutes.

breaths. Try to reverse the process when you come out of the pose. This will provide support and comfort.

4. Cobra pose (or "Bhujangasana"): Lie down on your stomach on Earth. With your palms facing out, place your hands near your chest. Keep your bent elbows straight and bring your sides towards you. Your toes should be tucked and your feet should touch the ground. Push the tops and palms of both your hands into the ground. Then, raise your chest up and lift your head off the ground. Your elbows should be straightened as you press upwards. As you engage your chest, keep your pelvis pressed against the Earth. Keep your head down and your gaze toward the sky. If it's in your practice, engage your hips. Sphinx pose, also known as "Salamba Bhujangasana", can be substituted if you don't have the pose in your practice. The alternative pose is to lie flat on your

stomach and your hands press into the Earth. Place your forearms on a flat surface, with your elbows bent. Place your feet flat on a flat surface. You can press down on your feet and forearms to raise your upper body slightly off the floor. Your hands and forearms must remain on the ground. Keep your eyes forward for a few seconds. No matter which version you prefer, keep the pose for five to seven breaths before releasing it to the floor.

Mantras to Balance the Throat Chakra

Sit comfortably in a comfortable, seated position. Take a deep breath in. Repeat slowly the following mantras.

"Sa Re Sa Sa, Sa Re Sa Sa, Sa Re Sa Sa, Sa Rung. Har Re Har Har, Har Re Har Har, Har Re Har Har, Har Rung."

The following is the translation of the mantra:

"The Total Infinite exists here and everywhere." God's creativity exists everywhere, here and everywhere.

This chart represents the creativity and the air in the Throat. It also connects the Divine of "sa," and the physical "har", to help you overcome adversity. It also helps you to eliminate any negativity from your body that could prevent your Truth from being communicated. It allows kundalini and other spiritual beings to rise up into the Crown.

"Aap Sahaaee Hoaa, Sachay Daa, Sachaa Doaa, Har, Har, Har."

This mantra's translation is:

"The Divine has become my refuge." The Creative Divine supports me.

This mantra helps to eliminate enemies and avoid animosity. It can also help you control your mind. It allows you confidence to venture into the unknown without fear and allows you not to be afraid. It is important to be aware of your negativity and the negative reactions of those around.

Chapter 16: Manipura Chakra Guided Meditation

Manipura (or the solar plexus) chakra is located just under your sternum, and above the navel. The force and energy behind your transformation will help you make the most of it in a similar fashion to how fire transforms material into light and heat energy.

Manipura chakra is about action, doing, and breaking through a pattern based on inertia, passivity, and inertia. Use a lighted lamp to meditate, or you could meditate in a circle with several lighted candles.

1. You can start by closing your eyes. Be aware of the rising and falling in your breath. Pay attention to the rhythm of your breath. Keep your attention on your breath and nothing else. Allow any distracting or intruding thoughts to slip

into your consciousness. If they do, acknowledge them gently and allow them the space to pass. Focus on the here and now. The only thing you have is now. You can't fixate on the future. Transformation and changes happen in the now.

2. Now imagine your right thumb being a bright orange flame. It flickers at what is called the epicenter of your existence. Watch the orange-yellow flame glow brighter and bigger with each inhalation. It radiates its warmth from the body's solarplexus region. The warmth of this flame is surrounding you from the inside.

3. Now imagine that you have a lot of sticks. Now, write a sentence or word that doesn't have any meaning in your current life. This is something you would like to let go or remove from your life. Be free from those things that do not serve a purpose in your life. Forgive yourself. Avoid feeling guilty or regret. Release negative energy

that is harmful and unproductive. This will help you to replace it by a positive, constructive force.

4. Now, put each stick in the flame. Now, watch each stick catch fire and start to burn. Visualize wind moving into your hands as you watch each stick go up in flames and carry the ashes away. The ash is removed far from you, and it's not likely that you will ever find it again. Are you motivated to pursue your dreams? Are you confident and able to chase your passions, goals, and dreams? What is it that is preventing you achieving your dreams? What is causing you to be delayed in your fulfillment? Many times, we feel exhausted in one area of life and then feel dead in the rest. This hinders us from fully experiencing the life-changing wonders that await us.

5. Standing slowly and putting your feet wider than normal, you can stand up.

Reach your arms high overhead. Gently place your fingers together. Extend the pointer finger. Every time you inhale, extend your arms high so that your arms reach the sky. Breathe in and raise your arms. Keep your chest open and breathe out, while moving your arms across the legs. Do this for 7-8 times. Pause when you are done. You can also make a prayer gesture by folding your hands and placing it on your heart. Notice what it has done to you. It's likely that you have broken out of your cycle of lethargy and been inspired to take action. You can find a new force in you that propels you towards productivity and action.

Fire stands for action, power results, doing and is the symbol of action. It is the power of results, which can be achieved by combining and integrating forces instead of trying to gain dominance or take over. Remember grace and simplicity can be real power. You are far more powerful, dynamic, and complete that you imagine. You are greater than all forces.

Chapter 17: Kundalini Meditation

Kundalini meditations are great for facilitating a complete awakening.

How to Use It

This meditation is not recommended for those who are just starting to awaken their Kundalini energy. This meditation is shorter and you can get to know Kundalini energy better before you move on to the longer meditation. For support in the event that you feel any of these symptoms, you may want to connect with Kundalini awakeners nearby. These symptoms can be both joyful and empowering, but they can also be overwhelming. Talking with others and sharing your experiences can help you to feel more supported during this process.

Begin the meditation by lying down in an easy posture once you are comfortable. Cross your legs, squat down, and hold your head high. You should relax your eyes as you enter this meditation. You should not be distracted or interrupted throughout this process.

Meditation

Begin to relax and breathe slowly and deeply. To increase the time you take to breathe, make sure that you're only inhaling for four seconds before exhaling for four. You should focus on expanding your stomach and pressing your navel towards your spine. As you breathe out, you should shrink your stomach and pull your navel toward your spine. Your breath should flow easily and comfortably from one point to the next.

Continue to breathe, focusing on the acquisition of a gentle, but powerful rhythm. In, two. Three. Four. Out. Two, three. Four. Again. Your body will synchronize to a powerful rhythm that allows you to receive life-force energy through both your lungs and your heart. You are now experiencing prana. While you continue to give your body this energy, focus on how it feels. Relax as much as you can and let the energy of the breath take over.

Feeling completely relaxed can help you shift your awareness to the root chakra. Notice the dense, powerful energy that lies at the base and spine. You can continue breathing using the four-in, four-out rhythm while focusing your attention on this region. Do not rush this section, just relax and remain focused. Soon, you will feel an increasing feeling of energy. Your Kundalini energy will start awakening as a result of your awareness. Use your awareness and your intuition to move it up your spine. Imagine a loosening coil moving up your spine, and then slowly gliding past your chakras. A glowing red energy may appear alongside the Kundalini as it rests within the root chakra.

Feel the energy rising when it passes through your sacral Chakra. You might feel the energy vibrating in the orange color. Notice the sensations that you are experiencing and the power you feel within your body. This sacral area is a good place to observe the balance of masculine/feminine energy.

If your Kundalini rises up to your solarplexus chakra, take a moment to allow your inner strength to grow. It will intensify and magnify as your own powers are awakened. Be aware of any sensations you experience as a result. A powerful yellow sensation may occur as your energy moves through the chakra.

Let your Kundalini rise, now, to your heart chakra. Feel the sensations in your heart opening up. This will allow you to experience the emotions and thoughts of your Self. Be aware of what you feel. The awakened power and sensations you feel now can be seen from your root chakra up to your heart chakra. You may also notice glowing green energy.

You can continue to draw energy up. Now let it flow through the throat chakra. This will allow you to feel the clarity of your ability speak your truth with love and kindness, as well as your ability to be yourself. This chakra can be seen as the color blue. You might also feel a strong, charged energy.

Now, bring the Kundalini energies into your third eyes chakra. Feel the energy rushing through your pineal and opening up your third-eye chakra. You might notice indigo energy when your third eye opens. You might also feel pressure behind your eye as the energy becomes more powerful, releasing a sensation you may not be used too.

You will begin to notice the Kundalini energies reaching your crown chakra as it continues rising. For a few seconds, imagine a violet lotus containing one thousand petals. You can now rest and let the petals open individually as your Kundalini awakens.

After the lotus petals have been fully opened in your crown chakra, visualize the Kundalini energies reaching above your body and connecting you to the source energy. Spend some time meditating, feeling the sensations, and paying attention to your connection to source.

Next, focus on your breath and return to it when you are ready. If you feel like your rhythm has been lost, you can refocus on breathing in and out at the count 4/4. Your navel should be pointed away from the spine every time you breathe in. Your navel should be drawn back toward your spine each time you inhale. This position can be held for as long and as many times as you wish. You will feel the Kundalini energy filling your physical as well as non-physical bodies.

Kriya yoga

Kriya yoga has been called the most spiritual form of yoga. It allows one to feel direct communion to God. This form of Yoga takes utmost discipline, dedication, and begins with prayer to invoke energy.

This style is not static because the poses they use are rarely able to give rise enlightenment. Kriya Yoga moves from one posture to the next like a dance. This is why it is often called "moving mediation". It uses deep breathing techniques and slow, controlled flow. These postures do not repeat mechanical exercises; they express the inner dynamics that is the eternal Self.

Kriya Yoga is different than Hatha Yoga in many aspects. The main difference being that Kriya Yoga does not focus on a specific physical program but rather an internal spiritual practice. It is intended for people who are in a certain stage of consciousness and must take extra precautions before they can attempt more advanced techniques.

How to Put It into Practice

There are five types kriyas. Each one has its own instructions. They follow the SatCakra-Nirupana's order for spiritual practices according to knowledge, time, space, body, soul, or both.

A. Shambhavi

The "Shambhavi kriya" is the initial kriya. It is a five minute asana that uses yogic respiration exercises to awaken the "Shambhavi," a dormant energetic channel that rises up from the base your spine to top your head.

You can inhale deeply through you nose. Keep your breath in while you exhale. Keep inhaling and exhaling as long as you can.

For five minutes, repeat this cycle and then go back for a further 10 minutes.

This kriya cleanses your nervous system and purifies your spinal fluid. It provides nourishment for every cell of the body. It is said to bring clarity and focus to daily life and can also heal imbalances that cause illness.

B) Chilaush

The next kriya can be called "Chilaush," or "Rajas -Kali". It helps to concentrate the mind on one mental object, such a mantra, visualization, and/or visualization of kundalini awakening. Concentration and energy are required to complete this exercise.

A blanket can be used as a cushion for your head. You will need to sit cross-legged and with your eyes closed. As you inhale out through your nose, imagine the day when it will be your last breath. Next, inhale through the nose. Repeat the process 10 to 20 more times throughout each practice session.

You can visualize yourself standing in moltenlava cauldron to do the kriya properly. As the lava smolders, you must keep chanting the Kriya mantra.

C. Bhramari

The next kriya can be called "Bhramari", "Ketu" or "Ketu". Concentrating on a mental object (e.g., your Guru's face) or a mantra is the key.

Crow Pose (Bakasana), or Crow Pose: Support your legs with blocks and lift your legs straight up to the sky, perpendicular your body. Deepen your breathing slowly and take in a deep, slow breath. Imagine your spine receiving the white light from Shiva. Do this for 5 seconds.

D. Bhastrika

The next kriya (or "Time") is "Bhastrika". It involves a series breathing exercises that purify the nervous systems.

In a comfortable position, place your right hand above your left. Next, exhale through you nose. Now raise your arms high without moving your upper bodies. The mantra is to visualize Shiva inhaling, and Shiva exhaling. The kriya must be done for 30 seconds at a time throughout the day. This is a great way to increase mental clarity as well as physical energy.

E) Anahat

The "Anahat" or the "Eyes" is the next kriya. It is a five minute meditative breathing exercise.

You can sit comfortably cross-legged and close your eyes. Take a deep inhale and exhale. After holding the breath for 2 seconds, exhale through your mouth. Visualize Shiva gazing on yourself. Keep doing this kriya for at least 60 seconds each day.

Chapter 18: Other Poses You Should Explore In Your Awakening Adventure

Ever sat down for a Kundalini meditation and wondered if it was right? You can do so many different positions and poses.

You may have many different positions or postures but most people who meditate will look the same. Meditation is one of the best ways to connect your mind and body and calm the mind.

Let's examine these meditational postures, and the exercises you can do to practice it correctly so you can deal with the 4-week long deep meditation program. Let's look at the various types of traditional meditation postures. Next, let's explore the types of practical exercises that you can do in order to prepare your body for those poses.

One of the most common images that people associate with meditation is the cross-legged position. This can be done on a mat or the floor. If this is your first time doing this, it can be uncomfortable. This is because you may not be used to sitting for long periods of time with your legs crossed. It's normal to feel tingly in your legs, or aches and pains in your back, especially if your posture isn't perfect.

Variations of the Sitting Down Position

There are many positions you can take on the floor. One of these is sitting cross-legged.

The Lotus Position

This is the most common form of meditation. The Full Lotus is where your legs are crossed and your feet rest on the opposite leg. Your thumb and index finger would touch one another, and your thumb will be resting on your thighs. This is the ultimate pose in yoga and requires your hips to be open. You can avoid muscle aches by doing some light stretching exercises before entering this meditational pose. To help with back or muscular pains, lean back against a wall. You can use a cushion to rest your head on if it helps. One leg should be extended at a time. Next, bend your other leg towards the same position. Take your time getting comfortable.

Conclusion

Kundalini awakening is a rare opportunity that not everyone has the chance to achieve. Even though it might seem difficult, look at the challenges as opportunities to grow and become a better person. There are many people who have been through activation, just like you. Reach out for help if necessary.

It is believed that Spirit has its own reasons to do things, and humans are simply following its leads. It communicates through many channels: events, dreams and synchronicities, which are meaningful coincidences, as well a variety of other means such as dreams, waking up suddenly, and so on. The more aligned with the Spirit the more blessed we will become. Therefore, do your best to grow spiritually and listen to what God is telling you.

Be calm when you feel like you have "sinned", that you are losing spirituality. It is possible that you have been allowed by the Spirit to move on from it in order to teach you valuable lessons. If you feel the need, don't be afraid to make a comeback. Even if it is obvious that you are a wise person, this does not mean you should never make mistakes.

The activated Kundalini symbolises our connection with the Divine. Although we can remain human if that is what we desire, we also have the opportunity to experience the Divine within our flesh. This is not a binding obligation. It's more of an opportunity for us all to experience and learn. You can take it easy and accomplish more of the things you desire if you so choose. You can accomplish more when you start now.

www.ingramcontent.com/pod-product-compliance
Lightning Source LLC
Chambersburg PA
CBHW071336120626
46546CB00002B/581